Hanging the Pirates

D1303174

by
Charles Gaulden

Hanging the Pirates by Charles H. Gaulden
Published by Evangel Cathedral Press
200 Evangel Road
Spartanburg, South Carolina 29301

Unless otherwise noted, all Scripture quotations are from the New King James Version of the Bible. Copyright © 1979, 1980, 1982 by Thomas Nelson, Inc., publishers. Used by permission.

Library of Congress Catalog Card Number: 00-090800
International Standard Book Number: 0-9679971-0-0

Printed in the United States of America

Dedication

This book is dedicated to the faithful staff at Evangel Cathedral and Evangel Fellowship International.

Hope Alexander
Jay Barker
Michelle Barker
Linda Bertling
Margie Bibb
Larry Braswell
Darin Bunch
Jerry Clevenger
Kathy Cox
Lisa Dillon
Clint Dobbins
Lee Fix
Renee Fix
Susan Gaulden
Nancy Gibbs
Beverly Henderson
Joey Holmes
Phil Holmes

Anne Hunt
Jan King
Bob Leverette
Roy McClintock
Evelyn Miles
Houston Miles
Pat Mitchell
David Powell
Rayna Powell
Linda Read
James Reese
Dan Schoolcraft
Ronnie Stepp
Jesse Webb
Joyce Webb
Karen Winchell
Hope Wolfe

Acknowledgments

I would like to thank John Maxwell, Lloyd Melton and Houston Miles for their kind endorsement of this book. Also my wife, Susan, and secretary, Lori Rhea, who made numerous proofings for me. My administrative assistant, Margie Bibbs, was always making helpful impacts on this project. Howard Ridings and Creation House provided many helpful points of information. Finally, I would like to thank Larry Braswell and Jerry Clevenger who had shared my initial vision for this publishing endeavor.

Table of Contents

Section

1

Trials

1

Hanging the Pirates

James 1:2-4
"My brethren, count it all joy when you fall into various trials, knowing that the testing of your faith produces patience. But let patience have its perfect work, that you may be perfect and complete, lacking nothing."

In May of 1718, a gang of pirates, under the ruffian leadership of Blackbeard and Stede Bonnet, held the entire city of Charleston, South Carolina, at bay. During their daring escapade, they pillaged a dozen ships and anchored in the harbor, while demanding ransom to free the port. The city was altogether cut off from access to the outside world. Business came to a standstill.

Blackbeard started calling himself *Commodore*, and assumed authority over his fleet of ships. He now considered himself the king of Charleston. His flagship was the 40-gun *Queen Anne's Revenge*, and on board with a ringside seat, was young Captain Stede Bonnet. Lieutenant Richards led the *Revenge*, Bonnet's former ship, mounting at least ten guns, and Israel Hands commanded the *Adventure*, mounting eight guns. Altogether, the flotilla formed a formidable enemy, strong enough to terrify any port city.

To compound matters, Blackbeard captured some key citizens and threatened their lives if the stated ransom were not paid. He was not bluffing. His rage touched everything. Families barricaded themselves in their homes in fear for their lives.

The citizens had good reason to fear. Blackbeard had threatened to storm the streets, ravage the residents, and burn the buildings. The whole region fell into the grip of piracy. The nearest protective warships lay more than 100 miles away. The pirates paralyzed the place.

Eventually, the circumstances did dramatically turn. The pirates gleefully left when their harsh demands were met. Never before had such a brazen act of piracy occurred in American history. The defenseless city was taken completely by surprise this time — but never again!

This test of fortitude produced an amazing change. The good people of Charleston and of other Atlantic coast cities finally said, "Enough is enough!" They were not going to surrender their families and fortunes to a bunch of pug ugly renegades. Come what might, life would be different.

Before the year was out, all those cocky thieves who boasted of evil exploits were apprehended and executed. In fact, on December 10, 1718, virtually the entire township showed up on the boardwalk to watch Stede Bonnet swing from a rope around his neck. The day of his execution, he was taken on a long tour of the throughways so everyone could see the man who had once held them in such terror and so ruthlessly stolen their goods. This day he did not seem so frightening.

Bonnet's last words were, "Oh, my God! Oh, my God!" His body was left hanging for four days. A clear message was heard throughout all of pirate world. South Carolina was made of tougher metal than previously thought. She would hang pirates. Let the highjacker beware!

4

The title of this book is *Hanging the Pirates*. The words *pirate* and *trial* come from a common root. *Pirate* comes from the Greek word *peirate,* meaning *to attempt to steal.* Obviously, the pirate attempts to take something that rightfully belongs to another. The word for *trials,* however, comes from the Greek word *peirasmos,* meaning *to attempt to prove.* The Bible uses the term both in a good and a bad sense. For instance, the word can refer to the *tests* that are designed to make us better or to the *temptations* thrown to cause us to stumble. The same Greek word is used for *testing* and *temptation.* The trial can come with a heavy-laden ship of blessing into a safe port or as a buccaneer seeking to steal our treasure.

Trials can be sent by God in order to make a person stand while temptations can be sent by the enemy to make a person fall. The Queen of Sheba came *testing* the wisdom of Solomon. Also, Abraham was *tested* by God. In these two cases, the tests were attempting to prove the quality of wisdom in Solomon and the depth of dedication in Abraham. When King David was *tempted,* however, by his lust for Uriah's wife, the *temptation* ensnared him like a baited hook. One of the strongest weapons we possess is the power of choice under the banner of God's grace. We can choose to give into the trials and temptations of life, or we can choose to face life bravely and faithfully. The decision is ours.

Some of the spiritual foes which attack our peace, joy, and righteousness will be covered in this book as we study chapter one of James. We will sail up the first tributary of this St. James River and tackle trials, worry, discontent, temptation, selfishness, and others. One thing is for certain: these pirates will attempt to tackle us. We might as well go after them. **We can hang these pirates!**

2

When Pirates Are
in the Harbor

James 1:2
"...When you fall into various trials...."

The golden age of piracy, from 1689 to 1718, occurred because of England's unfair tax laws that encouraged smuggling in cheaper goods, on which no duties had been paid and no questions had been asked. By 1680, a piracy ring was operating regularly out of America. Wealthy merchants supplied and armed men to plunder ships of native traders and scurry home with luxury goods.

No golden age period exists for life's trials. They attempt to sail into our harbor all of our days. James was the great trial realist. He used the Greek word *hotan* in the subjunctive mood, which carries the idea, not just of possibility, but of inevitability. Trials must be spoken of in terms of *when,* not *if.*

One of the key principles of victorious living is rooted in correct expectations. If we expect to meet trials and meet them with a victorious attitude, then we will certainly overcome them. If we walk with a blind and naive perspective, then we will become disillusioned and discouraged with life's troubles.

Falling Into Trials

In 1716 a young, educated man named Edward Teach began his own adventures as a privateer sailing out of Jamaica during Queen Anne's War. We know him more commonly as Blackbeard.

In a day when most men were clean shaven, the pirate captain wore a large, jet-black beard beginning just under his dark eyes, covering his craggy face and giving him a horrible image. He wove his long hair in several braids, and before attacking a vessel, he stuffed lighted fuse cords under the brim of his hat. Doused with lime and saltpeter, the strings ignited slowly, encircling his head with swirling tufts of smoke, so that he mimicked a weird demon arrived from hades. Ships he stopped usually surrendered quickly.

Most of life's trials are not quite so flamboyant as Blackbeard. Instead, they come more subtly and well camouflaged. The Greek word for *fall* is *perippto*. The word is used in the familiar parable of the Good Samaritan. In the narrative, Christ tells of a man on his way from Jerusalem to Jericho who *falls* among thieves. They suddenly appear like pirates seeking treasure. He was so taken off guard that he lost his wealth, health, and almost his life.

Temptations can suddenly appear when we least expect them. First Peter 5:8 says, "Be sober, be vigilant; because your adversary the devil, walks about like a roaring lion, seeking whom he may devour." Winston Churchill gave similar advice in speaking before the House of Commons in 1913, saying, "We must always be ready to meet at our average moment anything that any possible enemy might hurl against us at his selected moment." No wonder he was called the *Lion of En-*

gland! Churchill, himself though, said that he was only the *roar!*

Various Trials

Between 1689 and 1718, over 2000 pirates harassed the American coastline. Confiscated cargo was brought into port and dispensed with the help of greedy tradesmen, anxious for gain. Dishonest officials made robbery on the high seas fashionable.

Pirates came like sharks from every corner, smelling the wounded prey's blood. Treasure flotillas, heavily laden with valuable goods at sea, attracted humanity's worst. Quickly, they formed a pirate confederacy, *The Brothers of the Coast.* Circling the victims, they stole millions.

Notice James 1:2 says, "...when you fall into *various* trials." The Greek word *poikilos* has the idea of *many-colored* or *many varieties*. Tests can be as varied as the 2000 pirates during the golden age of piracy. For some, the trial involves a troubled marriage, raising children, facing temptation, financial stress, forgiving someone, loneliness, or other stressful events. One thing these brothers of the coast have in common is ***they want our treasure!***

3

Valuable Treasure

James 1:3-4

"...knowing that the testing of your faith produces patience. But let patience have its perfect work, that you may be perfect and complete, lacking nothing."

Our greatest trials produce our greatest treasure. Valuable pearls began as an ugly irritant to the oyster. A tiny grain of sand fell into the thin crevice of the lowly oyster's home. He had no desire for such an irritating guest. As far as he was concerned, the grain of sand was a pesky little pirate seeking to steal his comfort.

The oyster had a choice. He could sit and stew about this intruder. (I suppose that would add new meaning to the term *oyster stew!*) Or the oyster could turn the irritant into a pearl. The oyster chose the latter. Each valuable layer of the pearl is a testimony to the oyster's persistent choice.

Jesus once gave a parable about a pearl of great price. In His day, pearls were much more valuable than today. His parable predates the invention of scuba gear and the modern-day

11

culturing process. Christ spoke of a pearl that was so valuable that a man sold all he had in order to obtain that single pearl. All the man owned was worth what once was the oyster's greatest trial.

When Paul was going through a most difficult time in his life, he asked God to remove the trial. Instead, God said to him in II Corinthians 12:9, "My grace is sufficient for you, for My strength is made perfect in weakness." Often God's greatest gifts to us come through our greatest tests. Why is this? Because trials are not the final word. God, and God alone, is the final word during difficult times.

Tests refine us, for they strip away impurities and leave the valuable. Which airline would be safe if planes were not properly tested? Which athlete could compete in the Olympics Games if he or she were not tested many times? All treasure is the byproduct of a series of tests. To obtain our rightful treasures of peace and joy, we have to set the mental sails of our ship, even against difficult winds.

Endurance

My next door neighbor was a Navy Seal during the Vietnam War. Everyone enjoyed having him as a neighbor. The families living on my street often gathered together for picnics and outings. You could not ask for a better place to raise your children.

Everything went well for years, until a divorced lady moved in with some rowdy, undisciplined teenagers. The kids mounted large speakers around their swimming pool and blasted loud music until one or two o'clock in the morning. Adding to the noise problems, evidence of drug selling began.

One day the speakers suddenly disappeared and, thankfully, the family chose to move on. Casually, I mentioned to Bob that the speakers had mysteriously disappeared. Sheepishly, he told how he had taken all he could take. One morning around 4:00 a.m., he put on his camouflage gear, climbed the poles, took the speakers down, and trashed them in the woods. I could only say, "God bless America for training such men!" Our hostage-held neighborhood was finally rescued by a Navy Seal!

During Bob's Navy Seals' training, he was put through the most rigorous ordeals imaginable. His final test was the famous *Hell Week* in which the potential Navy Seal was harassed beyond measure for seven days. They went without sleep, provisions, and rest — all designed to make some of the toughest soldiers America produces.

My friend told me the story of getting into water with his team of men and a heavy log being placed on their shoulders. The chief petty officer left them with these words: "Ladies, I will see you in the morning." All night long, they shivered together in the cold water and chilly night air, and never left their post.

Many days, they privately cursed their training, wondering all the while, "Why do all this stupid stuff?" But one night, all the training and all the testing would come into crystal clear focus. While on patrol on a dangerous island in Vietnam, they ran into heavy enemy fire. A conflict began, and they received incoming mortar shells. His best friend from childhood, Dennis, yelled, "Run, Bob! Run!"

It was too late. An incoming mortar shell exploded and Dennis died trying to warn his friend. Another shell slammed Bob into the river's edge, slicing countless metal fragments into his back, arms, and hands. His team was overrun by the enemy. A Viet Cong soldier stood over Bob and fired a round into him.

Only the months of training saved their lives. The team of Navy Seals, who had stood huddled together in cold water all night in boot camp bound to a splintered log, now faced the battle of their lives. The testing was not in vain. The enemy was routed, and Bob was taken to a hospital. He was told he would never walk again, and the use of his hand would be gone forever. But the training would never leave him. For one year he was hospitalized, and for one year he fought back each and every day. First a movement, then a step, then another. Today, he has the use of his legs and hands. Occasionally, a small piece of shrapnel works its way through the skin — a simple reminder to him of what he endured and the value of training.

Every Memorial Day, Bob drives to a lonely grave in Laurens, South Carolina. He always goes alone. He visits the grave of his friend, Dennis, and remembers the night he heard, "Run, Bob! Run!"

Does training make a difference in our lives? You had better believe it. Navy Seals trained by a heavy wooden log became united to a weightier log, called duty, honor, and courage. Training can build a Navy Seal, a marriage, a family, a church, and even a nation. James says that the testing of our faith produces a treasure called *endurance*.

Maturity

Another key treasure that the testing of our faith produces is *maturity*. The New King James translation says, *perfect and complete*. The treasure is not perfect in the sense of *without all imperfections*. None of us can claim such perfection. Rather, James is speaking of a maturity that allows us to be constantly moving forward in the things of God.

A good example is Abraham. He is called the *Father of Faith*. One cannot achieve a more mature stature than the *Father of Faith*. Abraham certainly was not without some imperfections. Rather, he had reached a state of maturity in constantly journeying forward with God.

How did he reach this maturity? One important avenue was the testing process. Abraham faced many challenges: emigration, enemies, family conflict with his nephew, Pharaoh's harassment of his wife, the paternity issue over Ishmael, and the offering of Isaac. Some of these tests Abraham passed, and others he failed. In them all, he moved forward in God.

In ancient times, wineries had a special process to make *mature wine,* or *sweet wine,* as it is called. To make sweet wine the juice was poured from vessel to vessel. Each pouring left some of the dregs in the bottom of the previous vessel. When the wine was sufficiently tested, then the result was a mature, sweet wine.

Jeremiah used this analogy in prophesying to the nation of Moab. He said in Jeremiah 48:11, "Moab has been at ease from his youth; he has settled on his dregs, and has not been emptied from vessel to vessel, nor has he gone into captivity. Therefore his taste remained in him, and his scent has not changed." In other words, Moab had no spiritual maturity because they had not been tested.

The first miracle that Jesus performed was the turning of water into wine at the wedding in Cana. One of the amazing aspects of the miracle was the fact that the wine was a mature, sweet flavor. The miracle produced a premium beverage for the wedding. One of the great miracles that Christ is producing for His bride, the church, is a more mature and pleasant character in all of us.

Johannes Kepler, German astronomer and philosopher born in 1571, was noted for formulating and verifying the three laws of planetary motion, now known as Kepler's Laws. Today, his work still serves as the foundation of much of modern space exploration. Though Kepler's Laws were later proven true, he was unappreciated during his lifetime. Most of the world had not yet accepted Copernicus' truth that the earth revolved around the sun, and thus rejected Kepler as well.

At his death in 1630, a close friend asked him if he were bitter because his work was not being accepted. Kepler responded, "God waited 5,000 years for one of His creatures to discover the admirable laws which He has given to the stars, and cannot I wait also until justice is done me?" Now that is mature, sweet wine. Kepler easily could have been soured by life's bitter dregs. Instead, he poured the trial into a new vessel, left the dregs behind, and moved on. ***What a treasure!***

4

The Hangman's Rope

James 1:2
"My brethren, count it all joy...."

"James, have you lost your mind?" This is the great question we would like to ask anyone who remotely mentions joy and trials in the same breath. Joy and trials go together about as well as women and mice. Anyone who has walked through anything knows that trials are no picnic. What is swimming upstream in this St. James River?

First, let us examine what James is *not* saying. He is *not* saying that we should have a giddy, careless approach to life. Isaiah prophesied that the Christ would be "...a man of sorrow and one acquainted with grief." Also, I Corinthians 12:26 says, "And if one member suffers, all the members suffer...." In other words, we all are to understand the natural trials that people go through and show understanding and compassion during those troublesome times. James is not promoting trials, but the proper attitude during trials.

Count It

James uses the Greek word *hegeomai* for *count it* all joy. The word gives the idea of *looking forward*. The word can

17

mean *to lead the mind forward.* A strategy session for victory is laid out in this Greek term.

James is saying we do not have to enjoy trials. Thank God. Instead, he is giving us good advice to look beyond the immediate and see what will come as a result of what we are going through. While this is easier said than done, the mind can be led forward.

We see where Christ led His mind forward in facing crucifixion. Hebrews 12:2 says, "Looking unto Jesus, the author and finisher of our faith, who for the joy that was set before Him endured the cross, despising the shame, and has sat down at the right hand of the throne of God." The way Christ endured the horrors of crucifixion was to lead His mind forward to the joy that awaited Him.

Paul also led his mind forward when facing relentless persecution to see that God was still in control. Romans 8:28 says, "And we know that all things work together for good to those who love God, to those who are the called according to His purpose." Paul convinced his spirit that God had the ability to bring good even out of bad situations.

Trials of our faith can be like plows that cut deeper channels in us for more of God's blessing to flow through us. During the ordeal, troubles are crushing. Literally, we feel turned inside out. Often, we have to take one emotional step at a time. The feelings, good or bad, follow whatever the mind has decided to believe about the affliction.

What I have personally found more helpful than anything else, is to start praising God for all the good that He will one day accomplish because of this unpleasantness. Praise is a rope that will hang self-pity and prevent its depressive moods.

Quit trying to figure everything out. Let your spirit go forward in God. He will set supernatural joy before you, and His joy will be your strength. His joy becomes a magnet that draws us to His grace and power.

Count It Together

Hanging pirates was not a solo event. The golden age of piracy waned when the colonies banded together and pursued their enemies. On November 17, 1718, Governor Spotswood of Virginia sent a team of 53 men under Lieutenant Maynard to take Blackbeard dead or alive.

Ocracoke Island, off the coast of North Carolina, had long been considered Blackbeard's headquarters. The region provided countless inlets for pirate concealment and many congregated there, avoiding capture.

Lieutenant Maynard arrived at Ocracoke Inlet as the sun was setting on Thursday, November 21. The mast of Blackbeard's ship could be seen just over the dunes in the last glow of the afternoon light. The *Adventure* was anchored where it always was, on the southern tip of Ocracoke Island. Since Maynard had no pilot who knew how to navigate the shoals, he decided to settle down and wait until dawn of the next day to attack.

At sunrise, Maynard approached the enemy. Realizing Maynard was going to board by force, Blackbeard shouted at the officers of the sloops: "Damnation seize my soul if I give you mercy or take any from you!"

"I expect no mercy from you. Nor shall I give any!" Maynard retorted.

Historian, Nancy Roberts, colorfully describes the battle, "A fierce hand-to-hand combat began as men slipped and slid in the blood on deck. Shouts and shrieks, the clatter of swords striking each other, and the sharp sound of pistols firing marked the fighting. Into the fray waded Blackbeard, wielding his great cutlass in an arc that struck the blades of the English aside. Maynard fought his way toward him until the two men met."[1]

When the smoke cleared, Blackbeard was dead. He had been shot five times and stabbed 20 times. Maynard ordered Blackbeard's head severed from his body and suspended from the bow of his ship. The pirate's body was thrown overboard.

Some trials take more than one stab or shot. They also require more than one person to tackle them. Ecclesiastes 4:12 says, "Though one may be overpowered by another, two can withstand him. And a threefold cord is not quickly broken."

Some of the remote Indian tribes of Peru make rope bridges out of common field straw. The bridges are strong enough to carry the weight of many men and animals. How do they do it? First, the women and children begin gathering the field straw and make the initial, small braided strains. Next, the men weave the thin strains into thicker ones. Each process produces a thicker rope until the main supporting cables are several inches thick.[2]

When James addressed this passage, he uses the words, *my brethren*. The Greek word, *adelphos* literally means, *born of the same womb*. James is speaking of those single strains who were born of the same womb of salvation. Woven together they become a strong enough rope to hang any pirate.

One of my favorite Scriptures is Proverbs 17:17 which states, "A friend loves at all times and a brother is born for adversity." I am sure some children have wondered if that verse meant their brother was born to cause adversity. While this may seem the case at times, the clear meaning of the verse is that a brother was born to help during times of adversity.

My eleven-year-old son, Benjamin, played little league baseball this year. He was the youngest in his age division. Hitting a fast-pitched baseball can be quite intimidating for an adult, much less an eleven year old.

We did all we knew to help him. We pitched balls, rented films, and even brought in a professional coach. Still the nervousness continued, to the detriment of his hitting.

One day, we noticed Benjamin walked to the plate and smiled at the pitcher. I pointed the smile out to my wife. We wondered what was going on. The ball came, and Benjamin connected. As he arrived at first base, he lifted his hands and mouthed the words, "Thank God!" Naturally, Mom and Dad were screaming their heads off.

Afterwards, we told Benjamin how proud we were of him, not only for hitting the ball, but also because of his positive attitude. He explained the smile. He said, "I decided to imagine the face of my best friend, Patrick Dobbins, on the face of the pitcher. It made me smile." He hung the pirate of intimidation with *the face of a friend!*

---

[1]Nancy Roberts, *Blackbeard and Other Pirates* (Winston Salem, North Carolina: Steward Publishing, 1993), p. 15.

[2]The *Discovery Channel* has a video on the Peru Indians making rope bridges.

Section

2

Double Mindedness

5

Seasick

James 1:5-8

"If any of you lacks wisdom, let him ask of God, who gives to all liberally, and without reproach, and it will be given to him. But let him ask in faith, with no doubting. For he who doubts is like a wave of the sea driven and tossed by the wind. For let not that man suppose that he will receive anything from the Lord; he is a double-minded man, unstable in all his ways."

When I was 12 years old, I went deep sea fishing with my father. On the way out, we had a grand ride. The fresh salty air and gentle breeze felt cool against the face and left a clean scent. The low-country scenery was seacoast perfect. One could not order a finer day.

Once the boat stopped, however, things began to change. First, I noticed my skin developed some moisture, not much at first, but moisture nevertheless. My head started feeling woozy. By now my stomach had a definite queasy sensation.

My worst fear had arrived — I was seasick. Fishing was impossible. I did bait my hook, but instead of fishing, I fed the fish. The worst case of the flu is the only way to describe the horrible illness.

My father said that my skin took on a pale green look. He said the color reminded him of bird-dropping green. I can't vouch for the pallor, but I certainly felt green. I lay down in the most central portion of the ship — anything to slow the motion.

By now, an African-American gentleman was as sick as I. I did not know until then that a brother could turn green also, though, with a slightly richer tint. The color is that nice antique green with a hint of mahogany. We both lay down on a bench, comrades in seasickness. Nothing like a good vomit to draw two people together.

We both tried to convince the captain to take us back to shore. He refused. Even our life's savings could not sway him. I was beginning to get desperate. Jonah's idea of being tossed overboard made good sense to me. The shore was about a quarter mile away in clear view. Maybe the sharks would give me a pass if I swam for it. The movie *Jaws* had not been created yet, so the terror of sharks was the last thing on my mind.

All during this gruesome time, my father was simply having a marvelous time fishing. He was an old Navy man from World War II. He had adjusted to the sea a long time ago. For him, the outing was a smooth day. For me, smoothness lay only on solid ground.

Motion Wellness

The passage before us speaks of being tossed to and fro by the waves of the sea. The passage describes a spiritual version of what we call *motion sickness,* first coined in 1881 by Dr. J.A. Irwin to provide a general designation for such similar syndromes as seasickness and train sickness. The convenient term, imprecise for scientific purposes, has nevertheless gained wide acceptance and endured for over a century.

I have coined a new term that I call *motion wellness*. This term describes someone who can enjoy the ride. Instead of fighting the waves, he focuses on the horizon and enjoys the trip. His system adjusts to motion and develops an ability to remain whole.

Life has a way of sending unexpected motion, storms, and waves our way. Avoidance is absolutely impossible. A ship in a harbor is safe, but ships are not built for the harbor. If you travel this life, you will eventually have to get out into the real ocean of trials. The boat will rock back and forth, and waves will slap against the bow. We either become experienced sailors who enjoy fishing or sick passengers begging the Captain to take us back to shore. ***We can be whole!***

6

The Inner Ear

James 1:5
"If any of you lacks wisdom...."

D r. Patricia Cowings, psychophysiologist at NASA, is considered one of the world's top experts on motion sickness. A big portion of her job is devoted to making trainees sick. The astronauts affectionately refer to her as the *Baroness of Barf.* And you think you have a hard job!

When asked by David Wallis, reporter for the *Washington Post,* in a May 2, 1999, article, "What triggers motion sickness?" Doctor Cowings responded, "A conflict of information between different sensory systems. Unfamiliar motion can cause the eye and ear to tell you different things."

The Greek word for *double minded, dipsychos,* has the idea of a soul with conflicting information. The human soul can become like a cork floating on the water. First, it is near the shore; next it is away. The surrounding circumstances determine its outcome and happiness. Fickle environmental events become the waves that govern the happiness or unhappiness of the double minded Christian's state.

29

The Bible teaches, in a number of key areas, that we can have a divided mind. First, Deuteronomy 26 warns us not to try and serve God with **double hearts** — with one heart on God and the other on the world. Rather, we are to serve God with all our heart, soul, mind, and strength.

The prophet Hosea spoke of Israel as a silly dove that first flew to Egypt for help, then to Assyria (Hosea 7:11; 11:11). They had developed a divided soul. The inner ear had conflicting information, and the nation became spiritually ill. The anchor of their soul should not have been foreign countries, but God, who had become foreign to them.

Second, in the area of **doctrine,** we can have a double mind. Ephesians 4:14 says, "That we should no longer be children, tossed to and fro and carried about with every wind of doctrine, by the trickery of men, in the cunning craftiness of deceitful plotting." Sound doctrine, while not as glamorous as the latest craze, is the anchor of the soul.

Third, we can have a **double-face**. Psalm 11 confronts the deceitful quality of saying one thing to a neighbor's face and another thing behind the neighbor's back. While most of us have been guilty of this at some time in our lives, it is not an attribute that God is pleased with in our lives. We should conscientiously picture the person's face as if he or she were in our presence.

Fourth, we can have a **double-tongue**. Paul says in I Timothy 3:8, "Likewise deacons must be reverent, not double-tongued, not given to much wine, not greedy for money." Being double-tongued often shows up in money matters. A person agrees to a financial commitment, but then does not follow through. Whenever we move up in leadership roles in God's kingdom, our options shrink, for God requires more of us. If a deacon doesn't "deac" in this area, then he should not be a deacon. If an elder does not "el" in this area, he should not be an elder.

Finally, in our text of James, we can be double minded in the area of *faith*. With part of our mind, we believe the promises of God; with the other part of our mind, we focus totally on our circumstances. Worry sings the sour notes into this unbalanced ear, and whispers quiet fears that rob us of sleep and calmness of soul. Worry is like a rocking chair — it gives you something to do, but does not get you anywhere!

Balanced Ears

Motion wellness occurs when the inner ear can balance the surrounding turmoil. A counteractive displacement is trained within the inner ears that compensates for rocky movement and helps prevent nausea.

Wisdom is the balancing force of the spiritual inner ear. James says, "If anyone lacks wisdom...." Obviously, we all lack wisdom, and we all desperately need it. Wisdom is the solution for life's disturbing moments. No wonder that Proverbs 2:2 says, " ... incline your ear to wisdom...." The inner ear can be trained to incline to wisdom's equilibrium.

Solomon asked for wisdom, and his request pleased God (I Kings 3:9). For a period of time, the young king became the most celebrated, motion-well person on the planet. People traveled far and wide to hear him lecture on a myriad of topics. His tapes and books were on the *Middle East Best-Sellers List* for years.

God's only warning to Solomon was not to multiply his wives, gold, or horses — simple commands to remain at the top. Why these three areas? In a *wisdom shell*, they would cause a conflict of information to his inner ear. His wives would steal his heart from the true God, his gold would make him soft, and his horses would deceive him into trusting in his own power. The resulting spiritual seasickness caused Solomon to despair of life itself (Ecclesiastes 2:17).

Daniel gave two signs of the end time — an increase of travel and an increase in knowledge (Daniel 12:4). Man's travel has increased, but often in the wrong direction. Man's knowledge has increased, but not in wisdom. Today there are more suicides, divorces, murders, and wars than ever before. Knowledge alone is not the answer.

Knowledge is the accumulation of facts, while wisdom shows how to use that knowledge. If ever there was a point in history when we need people of wisdom, now is the time. The promise is made, that if we ask God for wisdom, *He will indeed give wisdom to us!*

7

The Horizon

James 1:5

*"...Let him ask of God who gives to all men gener-
ously and without reproach...."*

Vision plays an important role in healing motion sickness. The eyesight, when locked onto the horizon, results in less tendency to motion sickness. Looking
over the gunwale to see the horizon calms the spirit. The horizon places the motion in proper perspective.

Vision draws something good out of us. When Florence
Chadwick first attempted to swim the 24-mile distance from
Catalina Island to the California coast, a fog rolled in over the
ocean's surface, preventing her from seeing the coastline. Even
though she was very close to the shore, and her friends were
diligently encouraging her, she decided to end the swim. After
seeing how close she came to the shore, she said, "If I could
have just seen the coast, I could have kept on going."

The vision would have drawn the extra perseverance needed
that day. To Florence's credit she did return later and made a

successful swim from the island to the coast. The clear vision of the horizon made the second swim victorious.

Vision is seeing something that is invisible to others. James places his vision on the horizon of God when he says, "...let him ask of God...." You cannot get a larger and more beautiful horizon than the Almighty. Seeing Him looming over the vast universe makes all of life's problems seem small. When our spiritual eyes clearly focus on God, something of Him which is beyond ourselves draws forth.

The Navy discovered an interesting factor with sailors' eyes. Those who served on deck in the fresh air and sunlight, constantly looking at the horizon, had their vision improve. Those who served in submarine duty, confined to close quarters and away from natural sunlight, developed myopia. My father confirmed this truth. He served as a signalman during World War II and was constantly looking over the horizon to read an incoming signal. He said that his vision during that period was the best of his lifetime.

Are you serving God on open deck in the bright Sonlight, looking at the horizon of God's greatness? Is your vision at its best, or has life swamped you under a heavy load of care and do you feel like you are in submarine duty? Are your eyes too close to your problems? Does your way seem dim from discouragement? Below are a couple of points on God's horizon that, when focused upon, improve one's vision and calm the soul.

Generously

See the generosity of God toward you. The text states that He gives to all men generously. The Greek word for *generously* is *haplos,* meaning *singleness of heart.* He gives with a single heart. Double mindedness does not exist in God. He does not give a gift and then reconsider the gift.

Has anyone ever promised to give you something and then did not give it? Do you remember how you felt about that person? If you are like me, the gift or the money was not the real issue. The person's double mindedness and lack of forthrightness made you lose respect for them. God is not so.

God's generosity is extended to all men. The Bible says in Matthew 5:45, "...He sends rain on the just and the unjust." I remember having a church member misquote this text as if God made bad things (rain) come upon the just and the unjust. I was able to pleasantly ask her the question, "Is rain in the dry Middle East a good or bad thing?" She thought a minute and then said, "Good." The meaning came into clear view for her. God's generosity is given to all men. A smile came over her face. God likes smiles.

Without Reproach

See how God generously gives to you. The text says that He gives without reproach. The Greek word *me oneidizontos* for *without reproach* means *not looking for fault*. God certainly knows all our faults, but He does not place faults on the filter of His giving-camera lens.

John Maxwell tells a story from one of his early days of pastoring in which a gentlemen in his church transcribed his sermons each Sunday and then left the paper marked with all the grammar mistakes — no compliments, just corrections. Each Monday, John faced another week of this man's relentless faultfinding. To add insult to injury, the man gave nothing to the church.

I speak for all pastors: On Monday morning, we want people to tell us we were great! Lie about our sermons if necessary! Wait until Wednesday before telling us the faults. God waits till Wednesday. He gives on Monday.

The Greek word for *without reproach* also means *without a severe rebuke*. The same word is used by Paul when he wrote to young Timothy, saying, "Do not sharply rebuke an older man, but appeal to him as a father, younger men as brothers, older women as mothers, younger as sisters, with all purity" (I Timothy 5:1-2). The word *appeal* has the idea of *taking aside*. Invariably, Timothy must correct people involved in ministry — it is the nature of ministry. He is wisely instructed to take them aside and give them the instruction in private rather than a sharp, open rebuke.

God's nature is to give without a sharp rebuke. Certainly the Bible contains examples of God's sharp rebuke, but those cases clearly are the result of man's stubborn resistance to God's gentle, wooing nature. From heaven's horizon, God is looking back towards us with a single, generous heart. *__He looks with love!__*

8

Calming the Conflict

James 1:5
"...Ask, and it will be given to him."

Can someone win the war against physical motion sickness? This same question was poised to Dr. Cowings by David Wallis in his May 2, 1999, article with the *Washington Post*. Her answer was "Yes. We've developed a program called Autogenic Feedback Training Exercise [AFTE], which I think will be available to the public in a year or two. In 12 half-hour sessions, the program pretty much reduces motion sickness or eliminates it altogether."

She goes on to describe how the program works. "Autogenic Feedback Training Exercise is based on biofeedback and a number of other disciplines, including attention training techniques. We electronically measure the changes in the body when people experience motion sickness. We teach subjects how to keep their hearts from beating faster, how to stop sweating. When you learn to lower your heart rate, decrease your blood pressure and change your sweating responses, the symptoms go away."

Can someone win the war against spiritual motion sickness? After reviewing Dr. James's prescription, I am convinced we can. His AFTE program of attention training techniques are very similar to NASA's program.   Like the physical man, the spiritual man must be calmed. How?   By asking God in faith with no doubting.

The word *ask* is an imperative verb. James is giving a command, not a suggestion. He is not giving rocky advice, but an anchor for stormy winds and rough waves. There are no exceptions. He says in James 4:2, "...You have not because you ask not."

There are a number of Scriptures that state clearly that we must ask. Proverbs 2:2-6 says, "So that you incline your ear to wisdom, and apply your heart to understanding; yes, if you cry out for discernment, and lift up your voice for understanding, if you seek her as silver, and search for her as for hidden treasures; then you will understand the fear of the Lord, and find the knowledge of God. For the Lord gives wisdom; from His mouth come knowledge and understanding."

Jeremiah 29:11-14 says, "For I know the thoughts that I think toward you, says the Lord, thoughts of peace and not of evil, to give you a future and a hope. Then you will call upon Me and go and pray to Me, and I will listen to you. And you will seek Me and find Me, when you search for Me with all your heart. I will be found by you, says the Lord, and I will bring you back from your captivity; I will gather you from all the nations and from all the places where I have driven you, says the Lord, and I will bring you to the place from which I cause you to be carried away captive."

Matthew 7:7-11 says, "Ask, and it will be given to you; seek, and you will find; knock, and it will be opened to you. For everyone who asks receives, and he who seeks finds, and to him who knocks it will be opened. Or what man is there among you who, if his son asks for bread, will give him a stone? Or if he asks for a fish, will he give him a serpent? If you then, being evil, know how to give good gifts to your children, how much more will your Father who is in heaven give good things to those who ask Him!"

The believer's request for wisdom should be offered in confident trust in God. Unwavering faith simply believes that God is a sovereign, loving Father who will supply everything needed for enduring life's trials. The limitless God has limited Himself to our praying.

Missy

Occasionally I get asked the question, "How do you know that you are called into the ministry?" My response is, "I love fried chicken and my dog was born on Easter morning." Those, of course, are not my only reasons, but they do help.

My dog, Missy, is a lovable cockapoo who was indeed born on Easter morning. An older couple owned her for a period of time until they could no longer take care of her. They decided to sell her to a family with small children. We were the fortunate recipients of this bundle of joy. She is kinda' dumb, but everyone loves her.

Missy is absolutely terrified of thunderstorms. The older couple had kept Missy in an outdoor pen from a pup. When thunderstorms came, as a puppy, she was left alone and frightened. Those formative years left her psychologically damaged to thunderstorms. Her heart races, and you can see the sheer terror in her big brown eyes. It really is sad.

When the storms come, she wants her daddy — in this case, me. No one has told her yet, she is not my daughter. (I think the trauma would be too much for her. She thinks she is human.) Wherever I am, she comes looking. She might awaken me at two or three o'clock in the morning seeking comfort. I hear the scratch at the door and her whimpering voice saying, "Daddy, where are you?"

I get up and go downstairs. Missy gets into my lap and I start soothing her with my reassuring voice and gentle petting. Immediately, she begins to calm. I literally can feel her heart rate slow. In time she falls asleep, and the storm passes. The conflict is calmed. On one of these night watches, I heard the reassuring voice of my heavenly Father whisper to me, *"I will calm the conflict for you!"*

Section

3

Discontentment

9

"The Crown Jewels"

James 1:9-12

"Let the lowly brother glory in his exaltation, but the rich in his humiliation, because as a flower of the field he will pass away. For no sooner has the sun risen with a burning heat than it withers the grass; its flower falls, and its beautiful appearance perishes. So the rich man also will fade away in his pursuits. Blessed is the man who endures temptation; for when he has been approved, he will receive the crown of life which the Lord has promised to those who love Him."

The Crown Jewels of England have a fascinating history that spans centuries. During those many years, the crown jewels have often had an up-and-down existence. They were pawned, sold, stolen, beaten, melted down, almost consumed by fire, rebought, and remade. Today they are considered priceless. The value could only be spoken of in terms of millions. The security to house, guard, and protect them also costs several million per year.

This passage concerns the crown jewels of the Christian faith, namely inner contentment. Peace was part of the atonement of Christ. As He took upon Himself the crown of thorns, He took our thorns of discontent that we might know His jewels of peace. He makes a number of wonderful promises concerning inner contentment. In John 14:27, He says, "Peace I leave with you, My peace I give to you; not as the world gives do I give to you. Let not your heart be troubled, neither let it be afraid." In John 16:33, He says, "These things I have spoken to you, that in Me you may have peace. In the world you will have tribulation; but be of good cheer, I have overcome the world."

True contentment is rare. William Shakespeare wrote in his play, *Henry VI*, "My crown is in my heart, not on my head; my crown called content; a crown it is that seldom kings enjoy." Most ills in the world are rooted in an inability or unwillingness to be content. Discontent is a pirate that not only robs our peace, but sears the conscience with ungratefulness.

The pirate Charles Gibbs, whose name was for many years a terror to commerce with the West Indies and South America, was at last taken captive, condemned, and executed in the city of New York. He acknowledged before his death that his discontent led to his first murder and theft. At first, his conscience was aflame with conviction. But after he had sailed for years under the black flag, his conscience had become so hardened and blunted that he could rob a vessel and murder all its crew, and then lie down and sleep as sweetly at night as an infant in its cradle. His remorse diminished as his crimes increased. All his crimes were rooted in discontentment.

Most pirates set captured men adrift in a small boat or left them on islands where they often were rescued. Not Charles Gibbs. He ruthlessly slaughtered captured crews in cold blood. Estimates place his rampage at over 400 innocent people killed.

In his written confession before his death on March 11, 1831, he wrote the following concerning his struggles with discontentment: "How often when the fumes of liquor have subsided have I thought of my good and affectionate parents, and of their Godlike advice! My friends advised me to behave myself like a man and promised me their assistance, but the demon still haunted me, and I spurned their advice."

The pirate of discontent can only be hanged by applying the peace of God with gratefulness. Colossians 3:15 states it well, "And let the peace of God rule in your hearts, to which also you were called in one body; and be thankful." The apostle Paul had learned to apply the provision of Christ's peace to his own life. In Philippians 4:11, Paul says, "Not that I speak in regard to need, for I have learned in whatever state I am, to be content."

Walking in Christ's contentment is a learning process. James gives in this passage two great principles of inner peace. Both principles are connected to how we view our lives. To understand these principles, we will weave them around the story of England's crown jewels, for they prove a remarkable parallel to the Christian crown jewels. Inner peace far exceeds England's finest treasure and its security will cost our utmost dedication.

To understand the story of England's crown jewels, we have to understand three men: King Alfred the Great, Oliver Cromwell, and King Charles II. We will let these three men be the framework for *a far richer crown not made with hands!*

45

10

King Alfred the Great

James 1:12
"...The crown of life which the Lord has promised to those who love him."

King Alfred lived from 849 to 899 A.D. During his reign he united all of England against their common enemy, the barbaric Danes. Once the pagan Danes invaded an English town, they systematically burned the churches and monasteries, often killing all the educated people. As a result, the whole land went into a spiritual and educational darkness. The situation got so bad that in all of England hardly anyone could read Latin or Greek.

Into this dark backdrop, one man beaconed hope, light, unity, and victory. His name was King Alfred, and people still to this day call him *the Great*. He embodied what it meant to be truly a great king. He treated rich and poor alike. He valued all his subjects and held their welfare as his utmost interest. Through his heroic efforts, the Christian faith was preserved in England, ultimately spreading to America and other parts of the world.

Alfred wore a rather simple crown for a king. His crown was made of gold wire and inset with precious stones. What gave the crown real value was the fair and noble head that it rested upon.

The Heavenly King

The Greek word for *crown* in this passage is *stephanos.* The word described the victor's crown, won by victorious kings and athletes. Interestingly enough, it is the same word that was used in all four Gospels to describe the crown of thorns that sat on the greatest king that ever lived, Jesus of Nazareth. He who was rich became poor for us, that we who are poor might become rich in Him.

King Alfred attributed anything good in himself to the greatness of Jesus Christ. In like manner, our contentment is forever linked to our willingness to lean on the regal power of Christ. We are a royal priesthood, a holy nation, a peculiar people who should show forth the praises of Him who called us out of darkness into His marvelous light. One way we show those praises is by our countenance of peace.

The acclaimed University of California sociologist, Robert Bellah, says, "What is missing in our culture is a sense of connectedness to each other and to some great cause." Christ bought and paid for that connection. He purchased the greatest cause that anyone could ever hope to find in themselves alone.

To facilitate a common connection within the body of Christ, an invisible leveling must take place. While in Jericho, Jesus told the lowly beggar, Bartimaeus, "Arise!" A few steps later, Jesus told the wealthy tax gatherer, Zacchaeus, "Come down!" Both men received their sight that day. Lowly, blind Bartimaeus received physical sight, and Zacchaeus, his spiritual sight. That day, the low went up and the high came down. Both went home content and connected.

The crown jewels of the Christian faith are for the poor to see their wealth in Christ and for the rich to see their poverty. What a paradox. G.K. Chesterton says that, "A paradox is truth standing on its head shouting for attention." Truth is shouting, "Take all the poor areas in your life and see how rich you are in Him. Take all the rich areas in your life and see how poor you are in temporal things." ***The crown of Christ is contentment!***

11

Oliver Cromwell

James 1:9
"Let the lowly brother glory in his exaltation...."

After Oliver Cromwell came to power in 1649, the king of England, King Charles I, was beheaded. In his short-sightedness, Oliver Cromwell melted down King Alfred the Great's crown and sold the gold and precious stones. His leadership was so religiously tight that England could not breathe. Theaters and drama were closed, and anything of culture was struck down. The religious were leading, but with a poverty mentality. The sense of connection was gone. They could pull the rich man down, but not lift the poor man up. The sense of a greater cause was gone. England became disenchanted with this somber approach to life and restored the royal throne in 1665.

The Poor Christian

The text speaks of the poor man glorying in his high position. Literally it means for the low man to *boast* in his high position. We tend to think of all boasting as wrong, but in a number of places, the Bible tells us plainly to boast. We use the same expression in English when we say, "Take pride in your work." We mean, "Do a good job." The Bible is saying the poor should take pride in his high position. In other words, "Don't focus on what you do not have, but on what you do have in Christ."

We all have pockets in our lives where we are poor. Most of us do not have the physical appearance of a model, the athletic ability of an olympian, the mind of Einstein, the musical gifts of Mozart, and, let us not forget, the money of Bill Gates. We all have many areas where we are inadequate. We can either focus on what we do not have or what we do have.

Do you know what it is like to be economically poor? When my wife and I first married, we spelled poor with five zeros! We joked that the rainbows in our neighborhood were in black and white. Those with hearing aids were on a party line. In spite of these very humble beginnings, we were of good cheer because of the good news of Christ.

Jesus quoted in Luke 4:18 a passage from Isaiah prophesying of the Messiah: "The Spirit of the Lord is upon Me, because He has anointed Me to preach the gospel to the poor; He has sent Me to heal the brokenhearted, to proclaim liberty to the captives and recovery of sight to the blind, to set at liberty those who are oppressed." One of the great signs of the Messiah coming was the fact that the poor had the Gospel preached to them. The Gospel had the power to lift the common man.

The financially poor Christian must never look at his circumstances the same ever again. He was taken from a dunghill to a high hill; his filthy rags were exchanged for regal robes; his debt of sin was erased by heaven's grace; his lowly social status is now royal blood; his hopelessness now is hope; his burden of sin is now lifted; his feet once caught in a mire of clay are now set on a rock to stay. Yes, the low man is made high.

Most people have heard the inspiring story of George Washington Carver who as a scientist asked God to teach him about the lowly peanut. In time, he invented over 300 products from the peanut. Some of the products he invented have always amazed me, such as a synthetic marble. Imagine that — peanut marble. (I wonder if he had the marble in crunchy or smooth style.) What many people do not know is Mr. Carver was raised in the poorest of economic environments. In spite of his poverty, he carried himself with dignity. His secret was being inventive with what he had. Because of his positive attitude, he could find untold wealth in anything, including the peanut.

True contentment in life is accepting and believing in yourself. In so doing, we accept all that God has placed within us. Confidence is the fruit of contentment. Winston Churchill achieved national prominence through his activities in the Boer War at the age of 25. He was taken prisoner, but two weeks later he escaped. His enemies hunted him and even set a price on his head. Handbills were distributed that described the young soldier, journalist, and adventurer:

"Englishman, 25 years old, about five feet eight inches tall, indifferent build, walks with a forward stoop, pale appearance, red-brownish hair, small and hardly noticeable mustache, talks through his nose and cannot pronounce the letter 's' properly."

Churchill did not seem to mind the less than complimentary description, but he did resent the fact that the price on his head was only 25 pounds! Evidently, the folks at home thought the assessment low, too, because his exploits became widely known and he was heralded as a national hero and later won a seat in Parliament.

God has assessed your value in the highest of terms: the death of His Son. Trust Him. Place value on what He values. *He knows a winner when He sees one and you are a winner!*

12

King Charles II

James 1:10
"...But the rich in his humiliation, because as a flower of the field he will pass away."

After Oliver Cromwell died, King Charles II was restored as the king of England. To the credit of King Charles II and others, the crown jewels were restored. Wealthy businessmen had bought the previously sold jewels and now brought them to be restored into a new crown.

The cost of restoration was very expensive. Cromwell had sold the crown jewels for a mere 238 pounds. The cost of restoration would exceed 31,978 pounds. For all this restoration process, King Charles II was greatly admired by the people of England.

After the jewels were remade by famous jeweler, Robert Vyner, they were stolen by a man named, of all things, *Blood.* He was described by a Lieutenant Evelyn on May 10, 1671: "The man had not only a daring but a villainous unmerciful look, a false countenance, but very well spoken and dangerously insinuating." Sounds like someone describing Lucifer.

In the theft, Blood crushed the crown and stabbed the king's loyal servant, 80-year-old Talbot Edwards. In spite of his wounds and age, Edwards arose and pursued the thief. Blood was apprehended and then placed in prison.

Shortly after Blood was captured, he was released by King Charles II and even rewarded. Something was very suspicious. In time, it became apparent that King Charles II had hired Blood to steal the crown jewels. The king wanted the prestige of restoring the crown, but he also wanted the cost necessary to restore them returned to his treasury. Apparently he planned to sell what Blood had stolen. He wanted to have his cake and eat it, too. Riches had deceived the king with discontent.

The Rich Man's Boast

James says that the rich man should boast in his low position. What does this mean? Real spiritual contentment comes from seeing how temporal material goods are. Charles Swindoll says, "The itch for things drains the soul of contentment."

Wealth can blind our perspective. In 1991, Barry Bonds of the Pittsburgh Pirates baseball team was offered $2.3 million, instead of the $3.2 million he asked for. Bonds said, "There's nothing Barry Bonds can do to please Pittsburgh. I'm so sad all the time."

One of the richest men in the world, oil tycoon Paul Getty was being interviewed in London. "If you retired now," asked a reporter, "would you say your holdings would be worth a billion dollars?" Getty paced up and down the room, mentally adding, "I suppose so," he said. "But remember, a billion doesn't go as far as it used to."

In spite of the enormous wealth and prestige that Princess Diana held, an apparent sadness surrounded her. In February 1989, she made her first visit to America. I was in New York City at JFK Airport the day she arrived and was privileged to see her disembark her aircraft. The weather was cold and raining, with temperatures near 20 degrees.

After seeing the lovely princess, we boarded our plane and headed for Africa. We arrived in the Sahara desert. The temperature was over 100 degrees. The scorching desert wind was stifling. From the desert, we flew to Nigeria and spent a couple of weeks among the remote villages of the Ibu people. I recall how extremely happy the people were in spite of their lack of material wealth. A boy took the tuna cans we had discarded and used them for wheels to make a toy truck. Pulling a string attached to the make-shift toy, he ran completely contented through the thick jungles.

James uses the image of the scorching wind that withers the flower of the grass and then is gone. He compares this image to wealth. How quickly the beautiful flower of England's princess was withered by death's desert winds. Yet how contented was a poor Ibu boy with tuna cans. Somewhere between the palace and the jungle, we live, and peace is possible.

How do we keep life in proper perspective? How do we live a contented life? One way is by not taking life so seriously. We are not going to get out of here alive anyway! I worked for seven years in the monument business. It is a dying business. The customers do not complain, though. I remember doing a monument for a woman named Ola B. Izzard. The amazing thing about Ola B., besides her name, was the fact that she lived to be 113 years old. Bending over that cold granite and carving the number 113 left a lasting impression on me. Even a long life ends. We need to make the most of the time we have.

The real hero in the story of England's crown jewels was Talbot Edwards. All of his life, he had served his country by guarding the valuable treasure. He had seen the crown pawned, sold, rebought, remade, crushed, stolen, and recovered. In the midst of such hypocrisy, Talbot Edwards could have easily compromised his service to his country. Instead, he kept his focus on his duty.

The crown jewels of Christ, purchased by painful thorns, have been entrusted to us. Over the centuries, they have been honored and dishonored, protected and pawned, restored and stolen. They have been placed in our trust for safe keeping. Contentment lies in our own hands. How we live does make a difference. May we join with the brave souls who said, *"For me to live is Christ!"*

Section

4

Temptation

13

Captain Hook

James 1:13-15

*"Let no one say when he is tempted, 'I am tempted
by God'; for God cannot be tempted by evil, nor does
He Himself tempt anyone. But each one is tempted when
he is drawn away by his own desires and enticed. Then,
when desire has conceived, it gives birth to sin; and sin,
when it is full-grown, brings forth death."*

In December 1991, the motion picture *Hook* opened in
2,197 theaters across America. The idea for the film germi-
nated a decade earlier. Screenwriter James V. Hart's son
asked the question, "Dad, did Peter Pan ever grow up?" Hart
responded, "Yes. Peter Pan grew up. We all did. We all ended
our childhood, we became lawyers, bankers, movie producers,
moguls, accountants, Wall Street Bankers. We stopped believing in those things we believed in as children."[1] Within an hour,
Hart had the core idea for the movie.

Originally, Disney talked of producing the film, but the large
budget drove them away. Steven Spielberg obtained rights to
direct the movie. The movie stages, nine in all, spilled over to

61

Culver City, including Stage Twenty-Seven, where the Emerald City scenes of the Wizard of Oz had been shot. The black and gold pirate ship spanned 84 feet in length. Pirate crews swelled to 150 in the cast from the seedier end of Hollywood. Shooting ran 40 days over schedule. The cost continued to climb until it hovered around the $75 million mark.

On opening day, movie critics sharpened their pencils. They unloaded on Spielberg. The critics shot the talented director with every weapon in their verbal arsenal. The fans, however, wrote a different story. They gave the film a 95% approval rating. The film was a success. Revenues exceeded $288 million. Income from Peter Pan toys and lunch boxes garnered extra income.

My family personally enjoyed the movie, which we have watched numerous times. One of our favorite characters is the evil villain, Hook. Dustin Hoffman's excellent portrayal of Captain James Hook exemplifies Hook as tenacious, crafty, and cruel.

Dangling Hooks

Enticement pirates a cruel ship. The Greek word for *enticed, deleazo,* has the idea of being "hooked." In English we speak of those who are "hooked on drugs." We call prostitutes, "hookers." Yielding to enchantments stabs addictive, painful claws in the yielded.

America hosts an addictive society. Fifty million Americans, or 25 percent of the population, use nicotine, mostly in cigarettes. Nicotine addiction kills about 390,000 people every year. The nicotine hook boasts the number one cause of death in America. In contrast, a major hard drug, heroin, kills only 3,000 people a year.

Ninety-two percent of us have some addictive connection with the stimulant, caffeine — including yours truly. Legend says that shepherds at a monastery in Arabia were surprised to find their goats jumping around and playing late at night, when they should have been asleep. The shepherds found that the goats had eaten berries from coffee plants. The wide-awake goats were getting a kick from caffeine. Later, the monks figured out how to brew the beans into coffee and get the same effect.[2]

That early morning coffee craving should give us all some small idea of what faces those who battle far more serious temptation hooks. Adultery, alcohol, drugs, gambling, and violence destroy the family unit. Experiencing caffeine withdrawal or losing a good night's sleep is one thing, but losing a family is everything.

Temptation has many stages and scenes. Its budget grows massively like the federal budget. Spielberg's movie costs pale in comparison to prices extorted by the real Captain Hook of life's snares. The box office in America exhibits a sellout today. Unfortunately, buying a ticket is easy, and leaving the theater is all too painful. ***Temptation's books cut deeply!***

---

[1]Joseph McBride, *Steven Spielberg* (New York, New York: Simon and Schuster, 1997), p. 410.

[2]Richard S. Lee and Mary Price Lee, *Caffeine and Nicotine* (New York, New York: Rosen Publishing Group, Inc., 1994), p. 19.

14

Never, Never, Land

James 1:13-15
"...When he is tempted...."

T he movie, *Hook*, stages in the mystical world known as
Never, Never, Land. Here, children idealize the days
away with games, parties, pirate skirmishes, flying, swimming, and loads of fun. Temptation bypasses Never, Never Land.
You do not grow old or fat. Sounds wonderful! Peter Pan lives
in the sweet by-and-by.

But we are in the nasty here and now. Traps abound and
consequences exist.   Notice that James says, "...when you are
tempted...." No mention of "...if you are tempted...."

Snares attempt to pirate everyone. First Corinthians 10:13
says, "No temptation has overtaken you except such as is common to man; but God is faithful, who will not allow you to be
tempted beyond what you are able, but with the temptation
will also make the way of escape, that you may be able to bear
it." The Living Bible paraphrases this verse, "But remember this
— wrong desires that come into your life aren't anything

new and different. Many others have faced exactly the same problems before you."

James uses the phrase, "each one is tempted," which emphasizes the universality of temptations. No soul vaccinates itself from enticement. The present tense of the Greek language underscores the continuing, repeated, and inescapable reality of luring. Oswald Chambers speaks of the common trait of temptation in his classic, *My Utmost for His Highest*:

"The word temptation has come to mean something bad to us today, but we tend to use the word in the wrong way. Temptation itself is not sin; it is something we are bound to face simply by virtue of being human. Not to be tempted would mean that we were already so shameful that we would be beneath contempt. Temptation is not something that we can escape; in fact, it is essential to the well-rounded life of a person. Beware of thinking that you are tempted as no one else — what you go through is the common inheritance of the human race, not something that no one has ever before endured. God does not save us from temptation — He sustains us in the midst of them."[1]

A Catholic nun, Sister Sarah, ran late to an all-boy's school mass. She quickly took a shower and put on her habit without anything underneath. As she stepped fast across the platform, her robe caught on an exposed nail. She tripped and fell over the altar rail. Her habit tore completely off, exposing her in front of 200 young boys.

The Father quickly assessed the situation and exclaimed, "Everyone, close your eyes! I'm going to pray that God will strike anyone blind who looks at Sister Sarah!" Everyone fearfully closed their eyes.

Two boys in the back whispered to each other, "What are you going to do, Robert?" "I don't know. What are you going to do, John?"

John said, "I'm going to risk one eye!"

Humans risk both eyes. Christ understands our nature. Hebrews 4:15, "For we do not have a High Priest who cannot sympathize with our weaknesses, but was in all points tempted as we are, yet without sin."

Responsibility for sin lies with mankind. James says, "...God cannot be tempted with sin, neither does He tempt anyone...." The Greek word *apeirastos* states emphatically, "God is un-temptable." The verb has been translated "unversed or inexperienced in evil." God and evil exist in separate dimensions that never intersect. The rays of the sun shine on litter, but remains unstained. The nature of the light does not change. The holy nature of God never alters in spite of sin's power.

Man's first instinct leans toward blame-shifting. When God questioned Adam about his sin, Adam's response was, "The woman whom You gave to be with me, she gave me of the tree, and I ate" (Genesis 3:12). And when God challenged Eve with her actions, her answer was, "The serpent deceived me, and I ate" (Genesis 3:13).

An expert at evading, man even accuses God. Proverbs 19:3, "The foolishness of a man twists his way, and his heart frets against the Lord." Man messes his own world up, then turns around and points to God.

Welcome to the genuine world. We face concrete tests. We live with active struggles. No amount of Christianity changes the pressure of temptations, only the faith in the midst of the trials will sustain you. Captain Temptation transcends the fictional Captain Hook. ***Through Christ we can resist temptation's power!***

---

[1]Oswald Chambers, *My Utmost for His Highest, An Updated Edition in Today's Language* (Grand Rapids: Discovery House Publishers, Edited by James Reimann, 1992), p. 133.

15

The Bait

James 1:13-15
"...But each one is tempted when he is drawn away by his own desires and enticed...."

In 1904, Sir James Matthew Barrie wrote the now world-famous fairy tale play, *Peter Pan.* In the fictional account, Peter Pan sliced Captain Hook's arm off and fed it to a large crocodile that happened to be passing by. The crocodile liked the taste of Hook's arm so much that it followed him from sea to sea, licking its lips for the rest of him. Barrie writes of the discussion between Hook and his assistant, Smee, concerning the crocodile's desire for Hook:

> *"'In a way,' said Smee, 'it's a sort of compliment.' 'I want no such compliments,' Hook barked petulantly. 'I want Peter Pan, who first gave the brute its taste for me.' He sat down on a large mushroom, and now there was a quiver in his voice. 'Smee,' he said huskily, 'That crocodile would have had me before this, but by a lucky chance it swallowed a clock which goes tick tick inside*

69

it, and so before it can reach me, I hear the tick and bolt.' He laughed, but in a hollow way. 'Some day,' said Smee, 'the clock will run down, and then he'll get you.' Hook wetted his dry lips. 'Ay,' he said, 'that's the fear that haunts me.'"[1]

Mankind enters the world with a severed arm of desire. Relentlessly pursuing him, sin craves all. With the fall of man came fears and hooks of enticement. Hebrews 2:15 states that man was "held in bondage to fear." Man's very nature changed for the worse. Jeremiah 17:9 says, "The heart is deceitful above all things, and desperately wicked; who can know it?" The Puritan preacher, Thomas Browne, said, "Our corrupted hearts are the factories of the devil."

Even the strongest of God's people felt the power of temptation. Charles Ryrie lists biblical people who were subject to temptation:

> *"Remember Noah's drunkenness? Or Abraham's cowardice and lying before a heathen ruler? Or Moses' self-exaltation which made him strike the rock and kept him out of the Promised Land? Or Jacob's stratagems? Or the patriarch's mistreatment of Joseph? Or Elijah's murmuring? Or David's double sin? Or Hezekiah's ostentations? Or Jonah's rebellious spirit? Or Peter's denial of his Lord? Or John Mark's defection? Or Paul and Barnabas' strife? Some of the noblest men of the Bible have not only experienced temptation, but have yielded to its power."[2]*

James places damaged desires as the root of temptation. James 1:14, "But each one is tempted when he is drawn away by his own desires and enticed." The preposition that is rendered "by" is from the Greek word, *hupo,* which carries the concept of direct agency. "By *[hupo]*" our own lust, temptation carries us away, not even directly "by *[apo]*" God.

The Greek word for *desire, epithumia,* refers to a deep, strong desire or longing of any kind, good or bad. Sin packages itself in an attractive and pleasurable form. Personal desires, born of self-interest, render us susceptible to improper persuasions. In the end sin devastatingly pirates men. Lot chose the rich plains of Sodom, but lost everything (Genesis 13:10-13). Samson broke ropes and Philistine heads, but sin broke him (Judges 16:25). The disciples cast out demons, but denied the Lord of Glory (Mark 9:28-29).

In William Shakespeare's play, *Macbeth,* the Queen of Scotland, Lady Macbeth, desired the title, *Queen of Scotland.* The present king, Duncan, stood in her way. Persuading her husband to join her, the two plotted and carried out the king's murder. Afterwards, Lady Macbeth had to live with her own conscience. In one scene she cries, "Out, damned spot! Out I say! All the perfumes of Arabia will not sweeten this little hand!"

Temptation should not surprise us. A young priest served in a confessional booth for the first time while under supervision by an older priest. At the end of the session, the mature priest took the novice aside and said, "When a person finishes confession, you have got to say something besides 'Wow!'"

One of the keys to victory over temptation interlocks with our desires. The same Greek word for *desire* in James 1:14 is the same word for *desire* in Luke 22:15, "Then He said to them, 'With fervent *desire* I have desired to eat this Passover with you before I suffer.'" Christ nourished His yearnings for God's kingdom and quenched those for the world. We can do the same. William Barclay states it well, "A man can so hand himself over to Christ and be so engaged on good things that there is no time or place left for evil desire. It is idle hands for which Satan finds mischief to do; it is the unexercised mind and the uncommitted heart which are vulnerable."[3]

God can give us the proper desires. Psalm 37:4, "Delight yourself also in the Lord, and He shall give you the desires of your heart." I have often heard people quote the verse as if God will give them what they want. Now that is a dangerous thought! Instead, I think it is best to see God's redirecting our passion. As we delight in God's will, He gives us His desires. ***God's desires empower us to win over temptation!***

[1]James M. Barrie, *Peter Pan* (New York, New York: Random House, 1987), p. 88.

[2]Charles Caldwell Ryrie, *Balancing the Christian's Life* (Chicago: Moody, 1969), p. 78.

[3]William Barclay, *James, The Daily Study Bible Series* (Philadelphia, Pennsylvania: Westminster Press, 1976), p. 52.

16

The Hook

James 1:13-15
*"...When he is drawn away by his own desires and
enticed. Then, when desire has conceived, it gives birth
to sin; and sin, when it is full-grown, brings forth
death."*

When I was in college, some of my friends and I were
discussing the topic of fishing. One of my friends
Terry spoke up and said, "I would like to be a fish for
just one day. You could swim underwater without scuba gear. I
think that would be great!" My other friend Randy gave an opposite response, "I would not want to be a fish. You could be
eating a jelly bean and suddenly you are caught up and dragged
away."

The Bible uses the same image of being dragged away for
yielding to temptation. Dietrich Bonhoeffer, in his book entitled
Temptation, describes how this works:

"With irresistible power desire seizes mastery over the flesh. It makes no difference whether it is sexual desire, or ambition, or vanity, or desire for revenge, or love of fame and power, or greed for money. Joy in God is extinguished in us and we seek all our joy in the creature. At this moment God is quite unreal to us, he loses all reality, and only desire for the creature is real. Satan does not here fill us with hatred of God, but with forgetfulness of God. The lust thus aroused envelops the mind and will of man in deepest darkness. The powers of clear discrimination and of decision are taken from us. The questions present themselves: 'Is what the flesh desires really sin in this case? Is it really not permitted to me, yes expected of me, now, here in my particular situation, to appease desire?' It is here that everything within me rises up against the Word of God."[1]

The Greek word for *sin, harmartia,* means "missing the mark." In theological studies most students even take a course called *harmatology* — the study of sin. How does one miss the mark? I remember a humorous conversation with another pastor about the word *harmatology.* He said, "My congregation doesn't need a study in sin. They have an earned doctorate in the subject!"

James uses the image of conception and birth to describe the process of temptation. Conception requires the participation of two parties. The word for *conceive, sullambano,* is derived from a conjunction that means *together* and a verb that means *to take or to bring. Sullambano* means *to achieve conception.* If sin could be placed in a mathematical, conception equation, this would be the formula:

desire + enticement x the act of the will = sin.

What practical steps can we take to overcome temptation?

74

Here are four:

- Submit to God and resist the devil.

James 4:7-8, "Therefore submit to God. Resist the devil and he will flee from you. Draw near to God and He will draw near to you. Cleanse your hands, you sinners; and purify your hearts, you double-minded."

- Flee youthful lusts.

Second Timothy 2:22, "Flee also youthful lusts; but pursue righteousness, faith, love, peace with those who call on the Lord out of a pure heart."

- Develop godly friendships.

Proverbs 13:20, "He who walks with wise men will be wise, but the companion of fools will be destroyed."

- Use the Word of God.

Psalm 119:11, ***Your word I have hidden in my heart, that I might not sin against you!***

<hr>

[1]Dietrich Bonhoeffer, *Temptation* (London: SCM Press, 1961), p. 33.

Section

5

Ingratitude

17

Navigating by the Stars

James 1:17

"Every good gift and every perfect gift is from above, and comes down from the Father of lights, with whom there is no variation or shadow of turning."

The sea has no highways. In ancient and even modern times, captains often navigated by the stars. Fixed points of light provide clear location and means of direction. Celestial navigation dates back to the earliest days of man's exploration of the sea. Leaving the comforting familiarity of the harbor, a seafarer learned quickly how to determine bearing. Gazing into the heavens he becomes a nautical Sherlock Holmes, finding clues for guidance through the wide-open, ever-changing ocean.

Perhaps the greatest celestial navigator and explorer of all time was Captain James Cook (1728-1789). Famous for his three great explorations of the South Pacific, the volume of his discoveries surpass all other early explorers. His mapping charts, so extremely accurate, gave military direction even during World War II. In 1768, as a lieutenant in the British Navy, he transported a group of astronomers to the recently discovered island of Tahiti. In June 1769 they witnessed the transit of the planet Venus across the sun. Tahiti provided the perfect viewing sight. How could they know to be at that point on the earth at that exact time? They were experts at celestial navigation.[1]

James, the brother of Jesus, speaks of a different kind of celestial navigation. In James 1:17 Captain James says, "Every good gift and every perfect gift is from above, and comes down from the Father of lights, with whom there is no variation or shadow of turning." James speaks of the core goodness of God which never changes. Gratefulness allows us to see the fixed points of all His gifts to us. Ungratefulness, however, like a cloudy night, blocks all glimmer of light. Groping in the dark, we see only man's changing goodness and gifts. As a pirate, ungratefulness towards God disorients our perspective of Him.

In June 1993 the police in South Windsor, Connecticut, pulled over motorists in larger numbers than usual. According to the Reuters News Services, a patrolman stopped a motorist named Lori Carlson. As the patrol car approached her, she wondered what she had done wrong. To her astonishment the patrolman gave her a receipt that said, "Your driving was great — and we appreciate it." The leaders of this Hartford suburb had started a new program to give safe drivers a two-dollar reward for obeying the speed limit, wearing safety belts, having children in protective seats, and using turn signals.

"You are always nervous when you see the police lights come on," said Carl Lomax, another resident of South Windsor pulled over for good driving. "It takes a second or two to adjust to the officer saying, 'Hey, thanks a lot for obeying the law.' It's about the last thing you would expect." The program succeeded in improving public relations. In time, motorists joyfully waved at law officers.[2]

Many of us have a concept of God as a patrolman writing tickets. A wrong conception of God tragically pervades all our thinking and behavior. In the end, ungratefulness points its negative finger at man's destiny. A.W. Tozer in his must-read book, *The Knowledge of the Holy,* opens with these words, "What comes into our minds when we think about God is the most important thing about us."[3] We all have a theology, i.e., what we believe and know of God. Our concept of God forms who we are.

Hebrews 11:6 gives us a good perspective of God: "But without faith it is impossible to please Him, for he who comes to God must believe that He is, and that He is a rewarder of those who diligently seek Him." The very core nature of God exudes goodness and reward! ***Gratefulness allows us to see God is at work!***

---

[1]Alistar Maclean, *Captain Cook* (Garden City, New York: Doubleday, 1972), pp. 29, 37, 41, 54, 57, 59, 106.

[2]Craig Brian Larson, editor, *Contemporary Illustrations* (Grand Rapids, Michigan: Baker Books, 1996), p. 58.

[3]A.W. Tozer, *The Knowledge of the Holy* (New York, New York: Harper and Row, 1961), p. 9.

18

Disoriented

James 1:17
"Every good gift and every perfect gift...."

According to the *Chicago Tribune*, on February 6, 1995, a Detroit bus driver ended his workday and headed for the terminal. Somehow, however, he made a wrong turn. By 7:19 P. M., he had not arrived. His worried supervisors started looking for him. The driver's wife stated, "He is on medication and might be disoriented."

For six hours, the 40-foot city bus and its driver could not be found. Finally the state police found the bus and driver — 200 miles northwest of Detroit. The bus was motoring slowly down a rural two-lane road, weaving slightly from side to side. The police pulled the bus over, and the driver said he was lost.

A police news release later stated, "The driver had no idea where he was and agreed he had made a wrong turn somewhere. Apparently this had not occurred to him during the four hours he drove without finding the bus depot."[1]

Ingratitude disorients our way. The Greek word for *deceive, planasthe, means to get off course, become disoriented.* Groping around in the dark with self-directed thoughts, we cannot see the shining stars of God's goodness. Basil (337-379 A.D.), the bishop of Caesarea, describes ingratitude's harmful effects: "Ingratitude is a nail which driven into the tree of courtesy, causes it to wither; it is a broken channel, by which the foundations of the affections are undermined; and a lump of soot, which, falling into the dish of friendship, destroys its scent and flavor."[2]

All human giving is marred by our very humanity. Compared to the stable lights of God's giving, man's gifts are weak flickers that can fool. Daniel Boone was once asked, "Have you ever been lost?" "No," he said. "But I have been a might bewildered for a few days." Some ways that man's giving falls short and bewilders us:[3]

- It may not be sincere.
- It may not be sensible.
- It may not be sufficient.
- It may not be suitable.

Ingratitude disorients our friendships with God and man. Parmenio was a faithful general under Philip and Alexander the Great. He had opened the way for them into Asia; had depressed Attalus, the king's enemy; had always led the king's vanguard; had been a man beloved by all the men of war; and all the glory and fame Alexander possessed appeared to come through the counsel of Parmenio. He had sacrificed two of his sons in battle, Hector and Nicanor, and another on suspicion of treason for the good of his country. Having become jealous of his popularity, Alexander was determined to take his life. Jealousy is the ugliest form of ingratitude. Cleander and Polydamus, Parmenio's most trusted friends, were sent to slay Parmenio, without even giving him a reason for doing so.[4]

Gratefulness helps us honor our past blessings. The Persian leader, Darius, before he was king, was on an expedition to Egypt. Here he saw Syloson walking in the marketplace in a glittering cloak, but Syloson told him he would not sell it, but would give it to him on the condition, that he would never part with it. Darius received it and in process of time became king. Syloson then came to Susa the palace, saying he was one that deserved well of the king, and sought an audience. Darius seeing him exclaimed, "O you most generous among men, are you he, who, when I had no power, gave me that cloak, which though small in itself, was yet as acceptable then as greater things would be to me now? I will reward you with silver and gold." But Syloson said, "Give me neither silver or gold, but give me the kingdom of my dead brother, which is now ruled over by a servant." And Darius rewarded him with a kingdom for a cloak.

Gratefulness is tied to our memories. Notice how many times in the Old Testament that the Scriptures say, "But you shall remember that it was the Lord your God who brought you out of the land of Egypt and not you yourselves." When the memory of Rev. John Newton was nearly gone at age 81, he used to say,[5] "Whatever else I might forget, I still remember two things: *I was a great sinner and Jesus Christ was a great Savior!"*

---

[1] Craig Brian Larson, editor, *Contemporary Illustrations* (Grand Rapids, Michigan: Baker Books, 1996), p. 12.

[2] Elon Foster, *Classic Sermon Illustrations* (Grand Rapids, Michigan: Baker Books, 1993), p. 501.

[3] John Blanchard, *Truth for Life* (Durham, England: Evangelical Press, 1982), pp. 53-54. Blanchard expounds these points quite well.

[4] Peter Green, *Alexander of Macedon* (Los Angeles, California: University of California Press, 1991), pp. 346-347.

[5] John Pollock, *Amazing Grace, the Dramatic Life Story of John Newton* (San Francisco, California: Harper and Row, Publishers, 1981), p. 182.

19

The Stars

James 1:17
"...Is from above...."

Various astronomers have estimated the number of stars. All estimates are incorrect and have been revived and increased throughout the years. Just for the sake of illustration, the following star data are used. There are at least 10×11th power number of galaxies, and each of these galaxies contains at least 10×11th power number of stars. The total number of stars is calculated by adding the exponents. This equals 10×22nd power, total number of stars. The number reads as 10,000,000,000,000,000,000,000.[1]

The Bible specifically refers to the innumerable stars and God's ability to name them: Genesis 15:5, "Then He brought him outside and said, 'Look now toward heaven, and count the stars if you are able to number them.' And He said to him, 'So shall your descendants be.'"

Jeremiah 31:37, "Thus says the Lord: 'If heaven above can be measured, and the foundations of the earth searched out beneath, I will also cast off all the seed of Israel for all that they have done, says the Lord.'" Isaiah 40:26, "Lift up your eyes on high, and see who has created these things, who brings out their host by number; He calls them all by name, by the greatness of His might and the strength of His power; not one is missing."

God's creation of the stars aids man in navigation. Similarly, His countless acts of goodness, like innumerable stars, beacon to man clarity and direction. Gratefulness discerns the signs of God's gifts and journeys forward with Him. The Magi, men of science and astronomy, saw the Christ's star and came asking the question, "Where is He who is born King of the Jews? For we have seen His star in the East and have come to worship Him" (Matthew 2:2). Seeing more than physical stars, they witnessed the glory of God's ultimate grace. They fell down and worshiped.

James says that God's gifts are *perfect.* The Bible describes the nature and activity of God as *perfect:*

- **His will is perfect.** Romans 12:2, "And do not be conformed to this world: but be transformed by the renewing of your mind, that you may prove what is that good and acceptable and perfect will of God."
- **His way is perfect.** Psalm 18:30, "As for God, His way is perfect; the word of the LORD is proven; He is a shield to all who trust in Him."
- **His word is perfect.** Psalm 19:7, "The law of the Lord is perfect, converting the soul; the testimony of the LORD is sure, making wise the simple."
- **His works are perfect.** Deuteronomy 32:4, "He is the Rock, His work is perfect; for all His ways are justice, a God of truth and without injustice; righteous and upright is He."

Even in the worst of situations, God stands near. His light often shines through hidden and unusual events. One of those amazing illustrations of this truth occurred on November 25, 1809.[2] The brig, *Negotiator*, struck an iceberg and the 21-member crew abandoned ship. Only Daniel Foss ultimately survived the disaster.

The small longboat capsized near a small rocky island. Foss, grabbing a 20-foot oar for buoying support, miraculously made it to shore. The half-mile-length and quarter-mile-width island lay completely bare of any vegetation, even a blade of grass. Nor did the seagulls visit. Foss, who for two weeks prior to the shipwreck had been reading Daniel Defoe's *Robinson Crusoe*, now faced an environment harsher than Crusoe's. His only possessions were a small knife and the long oar that kept him afloat. In spite of these meager circumstances, he was grateful to God to be alive.

Scooping rocky pools, he captured rain water. Searching the island, he discovered a small cave for shelter. Awakened by a strange barking, the island hosted hundreds of incoming seals. Using the 20-foot oar, he clubbed his victims. He learned to subsist on raw seal meat for five long years.

If anyone had just cause to be ungrateful, Daniel Foss had. Instead, he carefully marked each day by cutting a small notch in his oar. Each seventh day, he honored the Sabbath by worship and the singing of hymns. Meticulously over several weeks he carved the words of a hymn onto the oar.

Near the end of his fifth year, rescue finally arrived. A Captain Call of the ship, *Neptune,* was blown off course. Spotting the stranded sailor, Captain Call sent three of his men in a longboat to attempt a rescue. With no landing spot and a raging surf, freedom seemed impossible. In desperation, Daniel Foss grasped his prized oar and plunged into the violent waves. He swam with all his might. For the second time, a simple piece of wood kept him afloat and saved his life.

Captain Call examined the carved beam in amazement. Etched into hardened oak, marks for Sabbath, worship, and a hymn to God gave testimony of a grateful heart. Even in the worst imaginable place, God stood near.

Is your heart marked with gratefulness? Can you see His hand in the best and worst of times? Has ungratefulness clouded your view? ***His stars still shine!***

---

[1]Jean Sloat Morton, *Science in the Bible* (Chicago, Illinois: Moody Press, 1978), p. 13.

[2]Hal Butler, *Abandon Ship* (Chicago, Illinois: Henry Regnery Company, 1974), pp. 1-16.

20

The Compass

James 1:17
"...the Father of lights, with whom there is no variation or shadow of turning."

From the thirteenth century on, mariners have used the compass to indicate direction. The magnetic needle points in the general direction of the North under the influence of the magnetic field of the earth. The mariner's compass, a large magnetic type used aboard ships, has bundles of parallel magnetic needles attached to the underside of the compass card, which pivots about its center in a glass-covered bronze bowl. The bowl is hung in gimbals, and hence the card retains a horizontal position despite the pitching and rolling of the ship. Often the bowl is filled with a liquid, which reduces pivoting friction.

The constancy of God encompasses the child of God. The Greek verb for *giving* is a continuous present participle, indicating God's good and perfect gifts are continually being poured out. God's nature remains constant in this ever-changing universe we all live in. Malachi 3:6 says, "For I am the Lord, I do not change; therefore you are not consumed, O sons of Jacob."

In 1982 my wife became pregnant with our first child. We looked forward to the birth of this little boy and had picked out the name Jonathan. Unfortunately, my wife miscarried. I cannot begin to explain the spiritual struggle she went through. "Where is God?" she asked in desperation. Nothing I said helped. Days went into weeks with no hope in sight. She finally was healed the night Pastor James Beall spoke at our church. Pastor Beall read I John 1:5, "This is the message which we have heard from Him and declare to you, that God is light and in Him is no darkness at all." The sheer power of the constancy of God healed her. She could trust God again, for in Him was no darkness at all. She found true north.

Variableness characterizes all created things. James uses two astronomical terms to describe the changeableness of creation. The Greek *parallage* and *trophe* for *changeableness* and *shadows* both indicate the variation of heavenly bodies. The sun rises and sets. The moon waxes full and wanes to a crescent shape. Light reflects and refracts differently moment by moment.

Man also varies. With his fickle nature, he often loses sight of all his blessings. Ingratitude robs him of countless joys. The nature of man is ungrateful. Jesus healed ten lepers of leprosy, but only one returned to give thanks.

A soldier in the American Third Army was sent to a rest camp after a period of active service. When he returned to his outfit, he wrote a letter to General George Patton and thanked him for the splendid care he had received. General Patton wrote back that in 35 years he had sought to give all the comfort and convenience he could to his men, and added that this was the first letter of thanks he had received in all his years in the Army.[1]

To hang the pirate of ingratitude, we must frequently align

ourselves with the constant sunshine of God's goodness. The compass plant, common name for a large plant of the family *Compositae,* grows on the prairies of the central United States. When the plant grows in full sunshine, leaves borne on the lower stem and growing from the root tend to arrange themselves vertically in a north-south plane, giving rise to the popular name. By this means both surfaces are equally capable of photosynthesis. ***Facing God, we see light and worship!***

---

[1]Paul Lee Tan, *Signs of the Times* (Hong Kong: Nordica International, 1979), p. 1460.

Section

6

Aimlessness

21

The Captain

James 1:18

"Of His own will He brought us forth by the word of truth, that we might be a kind of firstfruits of His creatures."

On August 1, 1914, Captain Sir Ernest Henry Shackleton sailed from London's East India dock for the South Pole. His 28-member crew was attempting to be the first humans to cross the South Polar continent. Seven days later, World War I began. If the crew became stranded, the world would be too occupied to look for them. The two-year expedition proved to be one of the greatest adventure stories in human history.

By October 1915, the crew's three-masted wooden vessel, the *Endurance*, was hopelessly trapped in the frozen waters. The crew abandoned the ship before the ice brutally crushed and sank the vessel. They set up camp on a floating chunk of ice called a floe. For the next few months, the floe provided a harsh home.

The *Endurance* crew learned to survive on seals and penguins. They endured bitter cold temperatures of minus 100 degrees Fahrenheit. On two occasions, the deadly predator, the sea leopard, tried to kill them. The 1,100-pound, 11-foot beast almost succeeded in sinking his saw-toothed teeth into one of the men. Killer whales encircled the floes looking for seals or anyone that looked like seals. Life was harsh.

The captain saved the men's lives by a daring decision. They would attempt to sail three 22-foot boats to Elephant Island and ultimately one boat to South Georgia Island. Amazingly, they reached the uninhabited Elephant Island. Twenty-three of the men were left on the beach, which measured a mere 150 feet width. The remainder of the island jutted forth into steep cliffs. The men had to make the narrow strip of land home for five brutal months.

The captain and five other men would attempt to sail one of the boats 870 miles to South Georgia Island. A small whaling station was located on the northeastern side of the island. The captain promised to return. The men trusted their captain.

During the journey they were battered by gale-force winds up to 150 miles per hour and waves 80 feet high. They crossed the infamous Drake Passage, which is still described as "the worst bit of ocean on the globe." Miraculously they arrived at the southwestern end of the island. Their boat could not go on.

The captain once again saved the crew by a daring decision. He and two men would attempt to cross the 20-mile island by foot. In the 75 years that men had been coming to South Georgia, not one person had ever crossed the island. The crossing was thought impossible. The terrain and blizzards on South Georgia Island are considered some of the worst in the world. To save time, the team carried no sleeping bags. Their clothes were already thinning. The frigid temperature was lethal.

Captain Shackleton miraculously staggered into the whaling station on May 10, 1916. They had made it. Their last contact with other people occurred in December 1914. The captain immediately requested provisions for his men's rescue. The task was not easy. The ice had moved in. But the captain never gave up.

On August 30, 1916, Sir Ernest Shackleton and a rescue ship arrived on Elephant Island. The jubilant men proudly requested their captain to see their secured hut and personal items. He refused. The ice was closing fast. In an instant, the men left everything on the island behind and went with their beloved captain. What had moments before been so all-important, now seemed insignificant. They were going home.

Alfred Lansing's book, *Endurance*, tells the adventure. The book also describes the capable captain. With great decision of character, he chose each man. He provided a tenacious approach to survival. Quitting was out of the question. His men's lives governed his utmost priority.

The Captain of Our Souls

Jesus Christ is the Captain of our soul. James says, "By His own will, He brought us forth." He is at the helm of the ship. He chose us to be on His crew. Since salvation is eternal, an eternal Savior is needed. The Greek language in James expresses the idea of the deliberate and specific exercise of choice. God's will is the source and basis of new birth.

Never has a child been born by his or her act of the will. The child is the passive recipient of the will and action of the parents. In the same regard, new birth is the act of God. John 6:44 says, "No one can come to Me unless the Father who sent Me draws him; and I will raise him up at the last day." John 15:16 says, "You did not choose Me, but I chose you...." Jesus told Nicodemus in John 3:5-6, "Most assuredly, I say to you, unless one is born of water and the Spirit, he cannot enter the kingdom of God. That which is born of the flesh is flesh, and that which is born of the Spirit is spirit."

We bring nothing of value to the ship. Fallen man's problem is internal. The only solution to the problem is an internal one. Outward ritual and action are but filthy rags. Without Christ as pilot, aimlessness exposes the person to life's cruel elements. Aimlessness is a pirate killing with weapons of insecurity, loneliness, and fear.

Famous writer Ann Landers was asked in a *Saturday Review* interview, "What have you learned through the many letters you have received for your column?" Ann Landers said,

"I've learned plenty — including, most meaningful, what Leo Rosten had in mind when he said, 'Each of us is a little lonely, deep inside, and cries to be understood.' I have learned how it is with the stumbling, tortured people in this world who have nobody to talk to. The fact that the column has been a success underscores, for me at least, the central tragedy of our society, the disconnectedness, the insecurity, the fear that bedevils, cripples, and paralyzes so many of us. I have learned that financial success, academic achievement, and social or political status open no doors to peace of mind or inner security. We are all wanderers, like sheep, on this planet."

To an aimless world, Christ came seeking to pilot the way home to safety. He gives purpose. He gives direction. He is the navigator of eternal life. ***We all need this Captain!***

22

The Cargo

James 1:18
"...He brought us forth...."

Pirates steal cargo. The pirate mission statement is simple. *Pirates will use whatever means necessary to steal cargo.* One pirate by the name of George Wall used trickery to board ships. After a storm had passed, he maneuvered his small craft near traffic lanes. He deliberately disguised his boat to appear damaged from the storm. He then drifted aimlessly.

Passing ships sensed no threat from this tiny, aimless vessel. Benevolent crews offered safe passage to harbor. Little did they know that by daybreak they would all be dead. The pirates would systematically slay the crew while they slept.

Aimlessness is a small but dangerous pirate. Lack of purpose can lull the believer into the sleepy world of casual Christianity. Days roll into weeks and then into years. Countless crews of fruit-filled days die and precious cargo disappears. Montaigne said in his essay, "Of Experience," "The soul that has no established aim loses itself."

What is Christianity's cargo? In one word: life. Ephesians 2:4-5 says, "But God, who is rich in mercy, because of His great love with which He loved us, even when we were dead in trespasses, made us alive together with Christ (by grace you have been saved)."

First Peter 1:3 says, "Blessed be the God and Father of our Lord Jesus Christ, who according to His abundant mercy has begotten us again to a living hope through the resurrection of Jesus Christ from the dead."

Ephesians 2:12-13 makes an interesting contrast on spiritual death and life:

verse 12	verse 13
death	life
then	now
separate from Christ	in Christ Jesus
excluded from citizenship	fellow citizens
foreigners	members of God's household
far away	brought near
hostility	peace

Benjamin Disraeli said, "The secret of success is constancy of purpose." The former prime minister of England is correct. For us, the application is constancy of purpose to life. The Captain of our soul brought forth a cargo of life, which is ours in Christ Jesus. We protect that life through diligent faith and purpose. When people seek to dampen our vision, we stick to our high goals.

A bishop from the east coast visited a Midwestern college near the end of the nineteenth century. He made the comment to the president of the college, "Everything about nature has been discovered and all inventions were conceived." The president disagreed remarking, "Within 50 years men will be able to fly." "Nonsense!" exclaimed the irritated bishop. "Only angels are intended to fly."

The bishop had two boys at home who would eventually prove their father wrong. Their names were Orville and Wilbur Wright. The Wright brothers were right. The Wright father was wrong.

Your Heavenly Father is never wrong. The right Father says, "Mounting up with the wings of an eagle is possible in Jesus Christ." Dampeners, soured by skepticism, cry, "No way!" Minute pirates seek to creep aboard whispering softly, "High goals are not necessary." But Jesus says, *"Come soar with Me!"*

23

The Ship

James 1:18
"...By the word of truth...."

Salvation comes by the Word of God. James says, "...we were brought forth by the word of truth...." God's Word is the ship of salvation. Believers are born again, regenerated, by the power of God's Word.

First Peter 1:23-25 says, "Having been born again, not of corruptible seed, but incorruptible, through the word of God, which lives and abides forever, because 'All flesh is as grass, and all the glory of man as the flower of the grass. The grass withers, and its flower falls away, But the word of the Lord endures forever.' Now this is the word which by the gospel was preached to you."

In the fall of 1989, the Berlin wall fell. The evening news was filled with reports of communism's demise. The event sparked my curiosity. I began reading Karl Marx's book, *Communist Manifesto*. I remember thinking, "This looks good on paper, but it sure doesn't work."

At that point, I heard these words in my spirit, "The words of My Son work. I want you to compile them and take them to Russia." The mandate never left me. I began a grueling research and writing project on the words of Christ. In May of 1990, the book was complete.

Two weeks later, I left for a mission trip to the Soviet Union. The country was just opening to the Gospel. Traveling across the Atlantic from New York to Helsenki, Finland, I felt impressed to give one of my books to an older lady. She seemed pleased. Little did I know the chain of events this simple gift would spark.

Our trip involved three major cities of St. Petersburg, Kiev, and then Moscow. We delivered over $40,000 worth of goods to an orphanage in Moscow. A Canadian by the name of Fred Lewsinko approached me carrying the book I had written. The lady I had met on the plane had given him the book. He asked, "Are you the author?" "Yes," I responded.

His eyes moistened with emotion. "We have been praying that God would speak to someone to write the words of Christ and bring them to Russia." Fred worked with Orphan Relief Aid (ORA). He asked for my other copies. Orphan Relief Aid was interested in publishing the work in Russian.

In the interim, Fred gave an English copy to a Russian lady. I received a letter from her. She knew English and was saved reading the book. She then led over 30 other Russians to Christ. They met every Tuesday night for Bible study. They had no Bible, only the English book I wrote. The group met to read and then reread the words of Christ.

Orphan Relief Aid translated the book into Russian, printed thousands of copies and distributed them throughout the country. I still receive letters from people who were converted reading the book. What are the odds of all these events? I can only conclude that God wanted that ship in Russian waters.

The Associated Press released a notice in July 1999 that Blackbeard's pirate ship had been discovered. Animal bones recovered from the wreckage have been sent to the Illinois State Museum for identification. "We're trying to get an overall picture of what type of foodstuffs they had on board and how well provisioned the ships were," said Wayne Lusardi, the head archaeologist on the North Carolina team working to recover the wreck. The goal is to get a better understanding of daily life aboard the *Queen Anne's Revenge,* the 90-foot former slave ship that became Blackbeard's flagship.

As discoveries go, buried treasure is not being found. So far, the museum, known for an extensive collection of animal bones, has identified the remains of a cow, a pig, and a rat. Hard to take that to the bank.

Ministry, void of biblical truth, is a sunken pirate ship, full of useless bones. Sir Frederick Catherwood comments on this verse in his book, *Truth for Life:*

> "I would issue this impassioned cry: 'Never put yourselves into the position where you have to evacuate the message in order to accommodate the method! Unless the word of God is there, unless your work has about it the authoritative ring of scriptural truth, unmixed with the glamour, glitter and gimmickry of so many modern methods, you have no warrant for claiming for your efforts the promise that "Faith comes from hearing the message, and the message is heard through the word of Christ"'" (Romans 10:17). ***It is the Word of God alone that is the instrument of the new birth!"***

24

The Crew

James 1:18

"...brought us forth that we might be the firstfruits of His creatures."

In the Old Testament, God's people brought an offering to Him, a portion of the fruits that ripened first, these firstfruits were a foreshadowing of the coming harvest. In like manner the conversion of a believer foreshadows others who will come to know Christ because of the newfound faith in the believer. Evangelism is the natural result.

A genuine Christian possesses a certain fruitfulness that sets them apart from a sinful world. Max Jukes, a well-known atheist, lived a godless life and married a woman with a similar life-style. Five hundred and forty of his descendants were traced, revealing these findings:

- 310 of them died as paupers
- 150 were criminals
- 7 were murderers

- More than half of the women were prostitutes
- His descendants cost the state one and one-fourth million dollars.

To give a contrast, a man named Jonathan Edwards lived at the same time as Max Jukes. Reverend Edwards lived a Christ-filled life and married a woman with the same convictions. One thousand, three hundred and ninety-four of his descendants were traced to reveal the following:

- 13 of them were college presidents
- 65 of them were college professors
- 3 were United States Senators
- 30 were judges
- 100 were lawyers
- 60 were doctors
- 75 were army and navy officers
- 100 were preachers and missionaries
- 60 were prominent authors
- 1 was vice president of the United States
- 80 were public officials
- 295 were college graduates
- Some were governors
- His descendants did not cost the state one cent.

Our Heavenly Father brings us forth by His love and also His belief in us. On August 16, 1999, baseball player Tony Gwynn hit his 3,000th hit. Many people lacked faith that Gwynn would ever make his 3,000th hit. Even at his 2,000th hit, he began to show signs of gaining weight. Certainly he could not last another 1,000 hits. Gwynn's father, however, never lost faith. He encouraged his son with his belief that he would hit 3,000. On the fateful day in August 1999, Tony Gwynn did what his father said would one day happen. After the hit, Gwynn remembered the words of his then departed father. His father's love and encouragement had lived on.

Our Heavenly Father believes in us even when we might give up on ourselves. He brings us forth that we might be the firstfruits of His creatures. I like the word "us." Only two letters form such a beautiful and inclusive word. Together with the purpose of God we hang the pirate of aimlessness. ***In Him we have destiny and fruitfulness!***

Section

7

Anger

25

Walking the Plank

James 1:19-20
"So then, my beloved brethren, let every man be swift to hear, slow to speak, slow to wrath; for the wrath of man does not produce the righteousness of God."

Stede Bonnet invented the concept of walking the plank. For all the renown of this type of execution, Bonnet alone used the method. He apprehended the ship and then forced the victims to slowly walk out on a wooden plank into the dreaded waters below. Sharks, waves, and exhaustion finished them off quickly. Bonnet drew perverted pleasure from his new invention. Even among notorious pirates, Bonnet ranked high on the cruelty charts. At one point, bounty rewards on him exceeded those of the feared Blackbeard.

Major Stede Bonnet at age 28 launched his piracy career in the spring of 1717, the peak of the piracy period. The major owned a wealthy plantation on the tropical island of Barbados. He had a wife and four children. From the natural realm, piracy seemed an unlikely pursuit. Bonnet did not need the money. He craved the thrills. In contrast to piracy, life on Barbados was boring. Capturing a ship, killing the victims, and keeping the loot offered a rush. Barbados offered responsibility, marriage, family, and routine. Bonnet wanted more.

He frequently displayed anger in the form of moodiness and sulking. His unmastered anger eventually mastered him. Through piracy, he vented his rage through forcing others to walk the plank. Little did he know, during the short course of his piracy career, his life perilously inched forward on a plank of his own making — a plank called anger.

Uncontrolled anger captured Bonnet. He made the terrible mistake of teaming up with Blackbeard. The seasoned captain saw through Bonnet's spoiled and uncontrolled lifestyle. Blackbeard held contempt for Bonnet's lack of seamanship and leadership skills. Through cunning, Blackbeard gained control of Bonnet's ship. Bonnet must now go where his new captain led him. When Blackbeard held the city of Charleston hostage, authorities marked all his crew for death, including Stede Bonnet.

While Bonnet made repairs on the ship, a Colonel Rhett apprehended him and his crew. Rhett imprisoned Bonnet in the Charleston dungeon. Disguised as a woman, the young gentleman pirate escaped. Quickly, Rhett recaptured him again. Facing certain death, Bonnet finally humbled himself, repented of his sins, and embraced the Christian faith. Nevertheless, on December 10, 1718, Major Stede Bonnet died of hanging. His lifeless body swung from the rope for four days as a warning to others.

Bonnet lost his family and wealth. His uncontrolled anger even took his life. As he made others walk the plank, so his anger walked him to his grave. Even his newfound faith could not undo the reaping of the seeds of anger planted years earlier. ***Unresolved anger exacts a heavy price!***

26

Constructive Planks

James 1:19-20
"So then, my beloved brethren, let every man be swift to hear, slow to speak, slow to wrath; for the wrath of man does not produce the righteousness of God."

Wooden planks can be used for good purposes. A house, ship, school, or church can be framed with it. Planks need not be used solely for walking someone to a watery grave. Similarly, God created us all with the healthy capacity of anger. He did not create us as Vulcans, portrayed in *Star Trek* as pure logical, emotionless beings. God designed anger as an emotional gift. Contrary to popular thought, anger can be constructive.

The Bible gives a number of examples of healthy anger. The Hebrew word for *anger* is *aph.* The word is used both of the emotion of anger and the physical nose. God designed the physical body to react to the emotion. Of the 455 times that anger is mentioned, 375 of those references deal with God's anger. If God displays anger, the emotion cannot be sinful.

117

Moses also had healthy anger. After his return from Mount Sinai, he found the people of God worshiping a golden calf (Exodus 32). Aaron gave the lame excuse, "The people made me do it. I threw the gold into the fire and this golden calf came out." What a whopper of a lie! Aaron's passivity allowed the idolatry. Moses' anger enabled him to destroy the idol and rid the nation of its evil influence.

The prophet Nathan used an emotional story to arouse King David's anger, thus leading him to repentance (II Samuel 12). Nathan invented a parable about a wealthy shepherd who killed a poor shepherd in order to steal his one sheep. David, a former shepherd, naturally felt anger over such abhorrent behavior. Imagine his reaction when Nathan pointed his finger and said, "You are the man!" David's fresh-felt anger granted him understanding into God's perspective about his sin against Uriah.

Jesus felt anger over the money changers in the house of God. In the Old Testament, God made provision for the selling of animals for sacrifice. Greedy merchants, however, price-gouged the people beyond measure. The trading area in the temple comprised the average size of a Wal-Mart. Christ surveyed the situation, sat down, made a whip, and cleansed the temple (John 2).

During the 1960s, America faced many riot potentials because of serious civil rights violations. Thousands on both sides could have easily died in the protests. Doctor Martin Luther King, Jr., however, stepped to the forefront and used peaceful demonstrations instead of violence. He channeled his anger in the right direction. His constructive anger saved lives and changed a nation.

Drunk driving causes over 16,000 deaths in the United States annually. One comedian jokingly gave his solution for the problem, "Design a driving lane especially for drunk drivers. Create a single lane, forcing them to crash into each other, thus, no more drunk drivers."

A more constructive solution came in 1980 in California from a small group of mothers gathered over the loss of a 13 year old killed by a drunk driver. They formed an organization called MADD — Mothers Against Drunk Drivers — and have consistently lobbied for tighter laws and restrictions. Their victories in legislation have saved thousands of lives.

Anger can be healthy. Properly focused, anger signals a warning, motivates actions, confronts slackness, and gives needed energy for action. Ron and Pat Potter-Efron in their book *Letting Go of Anger*, give characteristics of people who use anger well:[1]

- Anger is treated as a normal part of life.
- Anger is an accurate signal of real problems in a person's life.
- Angry actions are screened carefully; you need not automatically get angry just because you could.
- Anger is expressed in moderation so there is no loss of control.
- The goal is to solve problems, not just to express anger.
- Anger is clearly stated in ways that others can understand.
- Anger is temporary. It can be relinquished once an issue is resolved.

Paul the apostle gives good counsel about healthy anger in Ephesians 4:26-27, "Be angry, and do not sin: do not let the sun go down on your wrath, nor give place to the devil." ***Managed anger befriends us!***

---

[1]Ron Potter-Efron and Pat Potter-Efron, *Letting Go of Anger* (New York, New York: Barnes and Noble Books, 1995), p. 14.

27

Destructive Planks

James 1:19-20

"So then, my beloved brethren, let every man be swift to hear, slow to speak, slow to wrath: For the wrath of man does not produce the righteousness of God."

Anger can also be destructive. The same wooden planks used for constructing buildings can also be extended over the boat's gunwale for a sick torture. In the 1976 Olympic games, two British sailors were so frustrated with their performance, they set fire to their yacht and waded to shore. Their anger destroyed an expensive craft.

Anger can also hurt the human body. Doctor S.I. McMillen, in his book *None of These Diseases*, cites 50 illnesses that can be triggered by unmanaged emotions.[1] Several research projects reveal a direct link with poor health and repressing and ignoring anger. A 20-year study linked increased rates of heart disease, cancer, accidents, and suicide with higher hostility scores. A 25-year study revealed that high hostility scorers were five times more likely to die by age 50 from all causes of disease than their low-scoring friends.[2]

121

The Bible gives examples of the danger of destructive anger. Adam's first son, Cain, through a fit of rage, murdered his brother Abel. Genesis 4:5-8 gives the account, "But God did not respect Cain and his offering. And Cain was very angry, and his countenance fell. So the Lord said to Cain, 'Why are you angry? And why has your countenance fallen? If you do well, will you not be accepted? And if you do not do well, sin lies at the door. And its desire is for you, but you should rule over it.' Now Cain talked with Abel his brother: and it came to pass, when they were in the field, that Cain rose up against Abel his brother, and killed him."

Not only did Moses display healthy anger, but also unhealthy anger. Moses was instructed by God to speak to the rock and water would come forth (Numbers 26). The Middle Eastern deserts trap water in sand dunes. Over time the sand hardens like rock. Experienced shepherds locate these water-encased rocks and strike them with a rod. The water flows freely. In the first experience, the Lord had Moses strike the rock. In the second event God commanded Moses to speak to the rock. The people easily could have given Moses the glory for his 40-year training in the wilderness. Instead, the God of Israel wanted His people to see the supernatural power of His provision this second time.

In his anger Moses struck the rock once again. His anger prevented a quality and quantity of life for him. As for quality, he never fully saw the promised land, except from Mt. Nebo's peak. As for quantity, his life ended prematurely as a judgment prior to the Jews entering Israel. James says, "The anger of man does not achieve the righteousness of God." Moses learned this lesson the hard way. ***Unrestrained anger presses us to walk the plank!***

---

[1]S.I. McMillen, *None of These Diseases* (Old Tappan, N. J.: Revell, 1984), p. 116.

[2]Matthew McKay, Peter D. Rogers, and Judith McKay, *When Anger Hurts* (Oakland, Calif.: New Harbinger Publication, 1989), pp. 23-32; and Redford Williams, *The Trusting Heart* (New York: Time, 1989), pp. 49-71.

28

Removing the Planks

James 1:19-20
"So then, my beloved brethren, let every man be swift to hear, slow to speak, slow to wrath: For the wrath of man does not produce the righteousness of God."

J esus speaks of removing harmful planks out of our own eye. Luke 6:41-42, "And why do you look at the speck in your brother's eye, but do not perceive the plank in your own eye? Or how can you say to your brother, 'Brother, let me remove the speck that is in your eye,' when you yourself do not see the plank that is in your own eye? Hypocrite! First remove the plank from your own eye, and then you will see clearly to remove the speck that is in your brother's eye."

How do we remove the planks? How do we stop from walking overboard on a plank of our own making? Below are a few practical applications:

Understand your anger style. We all react differently to the emotion of anger. Doctor Gary Oliver and Dr. Norman Wright in their excellent book, *When Anger Hits Home,* identify different faces of anger.[1] I have listed the names below and added a few thoughts of my own. Understanding how we react helps us manage anger more effectively.

Carl Cool Head seems not to experience intense anger. He usually is pleasant, but can be very stubborn in creative ways. He can be a sweet rebel. In a pleasant manner, he does what he wants to do. When you make a request, he smiles and nods approvingly, and then goes out and does what he wants to do.

Dan Deflector expresses his anger in such a way that those involved in causing the feeling don't even know about the anger. His anger comes home, and family members pay for others' mistakes.

Karen Keeper holds her anger until she is with people with whom she feels safe. Friends and family members hear her frustrations, often accompanied with tears. She has a hard time coming to terms with root problems in her own life, much less communicating her anger to the ones who offended her.

Randy and Rita Revenge like to vent their anger by evening the score. They have good, detailed, long-term memories. Also, they are patient and can wait for an opportune time to get even. An ad filed in the classified section of a newspaper read: Wedding dress for sale, never worn. Will trade for .38 caliber pistol.[2]

Sam Slow Burner does not get angry quickly. Rather, his anger builds through a series of frustrating situations. Co-workers often mistake his pleasant demeanor to mean his request can be handled later. They will get around to his suggestions in due season. Deep down though, Sam Slow Burner wants things done in a timely and orderly fashion. When the frustration level fills up, you know it. Sufficiently aroused, he becomes a mover and a shaker. Actually, he does some of his best work when he finally gets mad.

Tom Tinderbox feels his anger quickly. He rarely holds back. He focuses his anger on someone or something else. He flames quickly and gets over his anger quickly. Sometimes he doesn't realize his temper leaves its mark. When I was in scouting, we had to build a fire using only flint and steel. Not thinking of the ultimate repercussions, my friend started his fire on the porch of the scoutmaster's cabin. He almost burned the cabin down. Tom Tinderbox has burned a couple of cabins down, unintentionally, of course.

Stella Straight Shooter expresses her anger directly at the root of her irritation. She has no fear of the results of her shooting. I usually get along well with Stella as long as she does not use a big gun. Sometimes she uses a high-powered rifle when a water pistol would do. Occasionally, stray bullets go further than she realizes.

Listen more and speak less. James says, "...be quick to hear, slow to speak, slow to anger...." The pattern stands clear. The pace of mismanaging anger slows with quick hearing and slow speaking. The rabbis use a saying, "Men have two ears but one tongue, that they should hear more than they speak. The ears are always open, ever ready to receive instruction; but the tongue is surrounded with a double row of teeth to hedge it in, and keep it within proper bounds." Listening helps us fully understand the whole picture.

Give your emotions to God. One of the fruits of the Holy Spirit is self-control. The passions of life come under the authority of the power of the Holy Spirit. Open the gates to your kingdom and let God's kingdom rule over your emotions. If we give the Holy Spirit a chance, He will work on our behalf. ***The Creator of our emotions can also control them!***

---

[1]Gary Jackson Oliver and H. Norman Wright, *When Anger Hits Home* (Chicago, Illinois: Moody Press, 1992), p.14.

[2]*Preaching,* March-April Issue, 1993.

Section

8

Sin

29

Cleansing the Ship

James 1:21
"Therefore lay aside all filthiness and overflow of wickedness, and receive with meekness the engrafted word, which is able to save your souls."

Barnacles slow ships. The growth of *Branta leucopsis* on boats is known as *fouling.* The hard-shelled creatures hitchhike onto the hulls of passing transports. A heavy spread of marine crustaceans on a one-square foot area may exceed six pounds. On a large ship, the cerripedes can add as much as 600,000 pounds to the cargo's weight.

Barnacle fouling of a craft causes a reduction in its speed. Fuel cost increases along with a loss in time. A heavily fouled ship may need as much as 50 percent more fuel to move the same distance it would with a clean hull. Wind-driven galleons could slow by 50 percent from the water friction.

Not only do barnacles slow a ship, they also reduce the efficiency of its navigation. The tiny pests make the surface of the hull rough and irregular. Maneuvering becomes difficult and erratic.

The organisms can settle on any part of the ship that is below the surface of the water. In tropical waters, fouling on wooden-hulled sailing vessels may take a few months. In cold waters, fouling may take two years. While cleansing the ship takes time, effort, and expense, the benefits are enormous. Every dollar spent on cleansing produces several dollars in efficiency.

Spiritual Barnacles

Christianity is a religion of action. Healthy religious action must lay aside the works of the flesh. Every converted Christian brings into his or her new life spiritual barnacles that are inconsistent with it. Growing below the surface, out of public view, are the weighty matters that hinder Christians. The Bible calls these pesty little creatures "sin."

James says that we should, "...lay aside all filthiness and overflow of wickedness...." The Greek word for *lay aside* is *apotithemi.* The Greek verbs in this verse are in the aorist tense, making the action of *laying aside all filthiness* a condition for receiving *the engrafted word.* Before God's word can be fully received, we must be willing to lay aside hindrances to that receiving. The Bible illustrates this truth in a number of places:

Ephesians 4:22-24, "That you put off, concerning your former conduct, the old man which grows corrupt according to the deceitful lusts, and be renewed in the spirit of your mind, and that you put on the new man which was created according to God, in true righteousness and holiness."

Colossians 3:8-10, "But now you yourselves are to put off all these: anger, wrath, malice, blasphemy, filthy language out of your mouth. Do not lie to one another, since you have put off the old man with his deeds, and have put on the new man who is renewed in knowledge according to the image of Him who created him."

Hebrews 12:1, "Therefore we also, since we are surrounded by so great a cloud of witnesses, let us lay aside every weight, and the sin which so easily ensnares us, and let us run with endurance the race that is set before us."

First Peter 2:1-2, "Therefore, laying aside all malice, all guile, hypocrisy, envy, and all evil speaking, as newborn babes, desire the pure milk of the word, that you may grow thereby."

The ship is built. The cargo is loaded. The sails are hoisted. The wind is blowing. Everything is ready to sail forward. ***Have you cleansed the ship?!***

30

The Barnacles

James 1:21
"...Lay aside all filthiness and overflow of wicked-ness...."

Barnacles are shrimp-like animals protected by limey plates. The creature's scientific name is *Cirripedia.* The featherlike, curly legs inspired the use of the name. The shell-less larvae swims freely for a time, but eventually they settle on a hard object, such as the hull of a ship. Once cemented to an object, they remain fixed to it for life.

Barnacles' shells are *calcareous* — Latin for *hard shell.* The cuticle-covered animal secretes a hardening substance forming a protective shelter. Safely inside their home, they spread their legs as a net to catch food. They are tenacious hitchhikers. They have been found on light bulbs, bottles, phonograph records, nonstick frying pans, seaplanes, rocks, crabs, whales, and even the feet of penguins! The list is endless.

The sticking ability of barnacles has long intrigued the scientific community. The secretion hardens like plastic, even under water. Man's inventions cannot approach its adhesive and durability powers. Barnacle cement torched to 622 degrees Fahrenheit only softens. Chilled to minus 383 degrees Fahrenheit, it does not peel or crack.

Physicians in the dental field think the sea creature's super glue has promise. Not only twice the sticking power of man's best glues, the cement is highly resistant to tooth decay. Until then, the marine creature will continue to be merely a pest to mariners. The annual cost of cleaning ships exceeds a billion dollars.

The Sin Nature

The sin nature has staying power. Man has struggled with his own sinfulness since the fall of mankind. Sin comes with a high price tag. The breakdown of the family, crime, and wars continue to stagger under sin's heavy weight.

Is there hope? Would God tell us to lay aside sin if it were not possible? Ships can be cleaned and so can people. The Greek word for *lay aside* was used in ancient time to speak of washing the body. The spiritual body must also be washed.

What are we to be washed of? *Filthiness* translates the Greek word *rhuparia*. The root of the word is *ruphos,* which, when used medically, literally refers to the wax buildup in the ears. God admonishes us to cleanse even the small things that can clog our spiritual hearing.

When I prepare a sermon, I zone everything out. My children tease me that they can ask me anything during those times, for I am not really listening. "Daddy, can I go to Disney World?" They ask. "Sure baby," as I go on studying. My daughter, Melody, has sat in my lap, taken her hands and lifted my face out of a book, and placed her nose to my nose. "Daddy, are you listening?"

Sin can zone us out to God's voice. Imagine how much goes into our spiritual ears each week. Alarm clocks are set to radios. Automobiles are filled with CDs. The workplace is often a studio of worldly clamor. Home sees the average American watching 28 hours of television per week. The wax buildup is epidemic. God's voice is regulated to an occasional flutter.

How do we cleanse the wax? One way is to fast noise. We speak of fasting food — why not worldly chatter? Occasionally, I go on a three-day noise fast — no radio, CDs, tapes or television. Afterwards, the ears feel so good. I can actually hear God's gentle voice again.

In the fifteenth century, the Dutch introduced a naval punishment called *keel-hauling*. The unfortunate delinquent was hoisted up and passed under the bottom of the ship. The culprit almost suffocated from lack of oxygen. The blows to the body from the barnacles attached to the hull could be fatal. Blood from fresh cuts attracted sharks. When man encountered barnacles, usually the man lost.

What happens when people encounter your ship? Do they brush up against a clean hull? Do they find an effective faith? Or do they walk away bruised and cut by crusty forms of hypocrisy? Do you inspire hunger for God, or hunger in lurking sharks for disillusioned people?

A small group of people started attending a church I pastored. They came from a pioneering effort that had failed. The young pastor had blatant moral and financial barnacles growing in his life. He kept them well-hidden below the surface of the water. The church could not proceed forward with the weight of his sin. The whole mess came to light. When they first started attending our church, I could sense they were checking me out. For about three years, they sat back in scrutiny. In time, they learned to trust again. After a decade, their faith in ministers was completely restored.

How very crucial for each of us to take seriously the claims of Jesus Christ. We must keep short accounts with God. We need to come home to harbor for checkups.

James not only speaks of *filthiness,* but of *the overflow of wickedness.* The root word for *overflow, perisseuma,* is the same one used in the story of the feeding of the 4,000. We read in Mark 8:8, *"seven basketfuls of broken pieces were left over."* The open-air meeting place was left as clean as possible. The leftovers would serve as a blessing to feed others. James though, speaks of sin's leftovers. They produce no blessing. James is saying, "Clean the scraps up thoroughly and toss them overboard. *Sin will only slow you!"*

31

The Tools

James 1:21
"...And receive with meekness...."

Cleaning barnacles was no small task. The ship had to be heaved down on one side in order to expose the other side for cleaning. The whole process was called *careening*. The vessel was laid ashore, preferably on a steeply sloping beach, parallel to the shoreline and pulled over by means of tackles attached to the mastheads. Relieving tackles, running under the ship's keel, were attached to secure points on the exposed hull. The angle could then be controlled.

After cleaning and repairing, the vessel was brought to even keel. The ship was floated off on the tide, after one side had been cleaned, turned around to face the other way, and careened again so that the opposite side could be cleaned.

Careening tools were comprised of tackles, ropes, scrapes, hammers, and files. Without these tools, cleaning was impossible. The crusted barnacles were too tenacious. In a hand-to-hand tug-of-war, the barnacle wins. Faced with man's hardened tools, however, the hard-shelled pest loses.

Meekness

Conquering sin requires a major tool called *meekness.* James says, "...receive the engrafted word with meekness." The prerequisite to cleaning is meekness. Why is this quality so important? One major reason centers on the willingness to admit a problem.

Nikita Khrushchev and President Kennedy were having a vigorous exchange of strong opinions. Finally, Kennedy asked Khrushchev, "Do you ever admit a mistake?" The Soviet Premier responded, "Certainly I do. In a speech before the Twentieth Party Congress, I admitted all of Stalin's mistakes." Before we can get help, we have to admit need.

Many misconceptions abound about meekness. Many people imagine an undue, poor self-image type for the quality of meekness. A.W. Tozer though, gives a proper perspective:

> The meek man is not a human mouse afflicted with a sense of his own inferiority. Rather, he may be in his moral life as bold as a lion and as strong as Samson; but he has stopped being fooled about himself. He has accepted God's estimate of his own life. He knows he is as weak and helpless as God has declared him to be, but paradoxically, he knows at the same time that he is, in the sight of God, more important than angels.

The faces of only three men in the Bible were said to have shone: Moses, Jesus, and Stephen. All three men exemplified the beauty of meekness:

Of Moses, Numbers 12:3 states, "Now the man Moses was very humble, more than all men who were on the face of the earth."

Of Christ, Mark 9:3 says, "His clothes became shining, exceedingly white, like snow, such as no launderer on earth can whiten them." Matthew 11:29, "Take My yoke upon you and learn from Me, for I am gentle and lowly in heart, and you will find rest for your souls."

Of Stephen, Acts 6:15 describes, "And all who sat in the council, looking steadfastly at him, saw his face as the face of an angel." Acts 7:60, "Then he knelt down and cried out with a loud voice, 'Lord, do not charge them with this sin.' And when he had said this, he fell asleep."

The Greek word for *meekness* is *prautes.* English cannot capture the meaning in one word. My definition is, "Meekness is power under control." All three men mentioned above had meekness in their toolboxes. Their spiritual power was under control. The tool of meekness comes with a light to brighten the darkness. Charles Spurgeon said, ***"God puts the beauty of His own brightness on meek men!"***

32

The Cleansing

James 1:18

"...The engrafted word, which is able to save your soul."

Cleaning a ship took time and effort. A team of people was needed to accomplish the task. The stubborn barnacles put up a good fight. In the end though, the hard-crusted shells would be discarded into the surf. Their once cemented life was now tossed into the sea. The water washed them away.

God cleanses us by the word of God. Ephesians 5:26 says, "That He might sanctify and cleanse her with the washing of water by the word." Before the priests could enter the tabernacle, they paused before the laver, a mirrored basin filled with water. The laver was a type of the word of God. Through God's word, we see ourselves more clearly and find cleansing and refreshing.

James speaks of the engrafted word as the cleansing agent. Engrafting is accomplished by splicing a branch from one tree to another. The branch will retain its own distinctive fruit while receiving nourishment from the tree into which it was spliced. A scion from a sweet orange tree can be engrafted into a wild orange tree stock. The result will be sweet oranges. The same potential is true for the child of God. If we engraft a scion of Scripture into our spirit and nourish it through meditation, it will in time produce sweet fruit.

What are the benefits of receiving the engrafted word? Below are just a few:

1. **We become successful.** Joshua 1:8, "This Book of the Law shall not depart from your mouth, but you shall meditate in it day and night, that you may observe to do according to all that is written in it. For then you will make your way prosperous, and then you will have good success."

2. **We prosper in the areas of applying the word.** Psalm 1:2-3, "But his delight is in the law of the Lord, and in His law he meditates day and night. He shall be like a tree planted by the rivers of water, that brings forth its fruit in its season, whose leaf also shall not wither; and whatever he does shall prosper."

3. **We become filled with joy.** Psalm 63:5-6, "My soul shall be satisfied as with marrow and fatness, and my mouth shall praise You with joyful lips. When I remember You on my bed, I meditate on You in the night watches."

4. **We obtain victory over sin.** Psalm 119:9, 11, "How can a young man cleanse his way? By taking heed according to Your word. Your word I have hidden in my heart, that I might not sin against You!"

5. **We become wiser than our enemies.** Psalm 119:97-98, "Oh, how I love Your law! It is my meditation all the day. You, through Your commandments, make me wiser than my enemies; for they are ever with me."

6. **We can give wise counsel.** Proverbs 22:17-18, "Incline your ear and hear the words of the wise, and apply your

heart to my knowledge; For it is a pleasant thing if you keep them within you; let them all be fixed upon your lips. That I may make you know the certainty of the words of truth, that you may answer words of truth to those who send to you?"

7. **Our progress will be evident to all.** First Timothy 4:15, "Meditate on these things; give yourself entirely to them, that your progress may be evident to all."

How do we engraft God's word? Bill Gothard, of the Basic Youth Conflicts Ministry, gives five practical suggestions:

1. **Receive.**
   Accept the living word.
   Read God's Word daily.
   Select a passage.
2. **Memorize.**
   Write out the passage.
   Highlight the key words.
3. **Investigate.**
   Ask key questions.
   Do word studies.
   Check cross-references.
4. **Meditate.**
   Turn each word into prayer.
   Put into first person.
   Picture the concepts.
5. **Obey.**
   Write out the application.
   Check concepts and principles.

Test the resulting fruit!

Section

9

Casualness

33

The Lookout

James 1:22-25

"But be doers of the word, and not hearers only, deceiving yourselves. For if anyone is a hearer of the word, and not a doer, he is like a man observing his natural face in a mirror: For he observes himself, goes away, and immediately forgets what kind of man he was. But he who looks into the perfect law of liberty and continues in it, and is not a forgetful hearer, but a doer of the work, this one will be blessed in what he does."

Pirates used deceptive flags to lull potential victims into carelessness. A friendly nation's emblem, hoisted high on the flagpole, unassumingly flew until the cargo ship sailed within range. Quickly the pirate's mascot replaced the counterfeit, and the capture ended abruptly. In time, wary crews learned to keep a constant lookout, lest they become deceived and lose everything. A rotation of sailors took turns perched high in the crow's nest. With a strong spyglass, the vigilant observation determined life or death.

James speaks in this passage of deception and observation. The Greek term for *deceiving, paralogizomai,* was an accounting term meaning *to miscalculate, to cheat.* No one likes to be shortchanged by anyone. The funds rightfully belong to us and not some unscrupulous person. James adds an added feature to the word by applying it to ourselves. He says, "Don't deceive, miscalculate, or cheat yourself."

James then makes his point that hearing the word and not doing the word constitutes a self-delusion. A flag of God's kingdom flies with the hearing of His word, but the flag of self's kingdom flies over the actually doing of His word. In such cases, we in essence pirate ourselves. We lose all the fruit and blessing that comes from hearing and doing God's word. His cargo never reaches the harbor.

Rachael Wall, an American woman and notorious pirate, was hung for her crimes in Boston in 1789. Born in Carlisle, Pennsylvania, her parents raised her in the Christian faith. Rachael described her parents as "honest and reputable." She credited them with giving her a good education and teaching her the beautiful principles of the Christian faith. Her devout father offered family prayers each day. His children received Bible instruction and all his children turned out well, except Rachael. She confessed, "They taught me the fear of God, and if I had followed the good advice and pious counsel they often gave me, I should never had come to this untimely fate."[1] In the end Rachael pirated her own life.

James admonishes us to stay on the lookout. His expression, *prove yourselves doers of the word,* stands in the middle imperative tense of the word, *ginomai.* The proper translation interprets the tense, *continually keep on striving to be a doer of the word.* The self must constantly guard against carelessness in the things of God. We hear so much. We do so little. Herein lies the danger. ***Diligently guard against casual Christianity!***

---

[1]Myra Weatherly, *Women Pirates, Eight Stories of Adventure* (Greensboro, North Carolina: Morgan Reynolds, 1998), p. 74.

34

Careless Looking

James 1:23-24

"For if anyone is a hearer of the word, and not a doer, he is like a man observing his natural face in a mirror: For he observes himself, goes away, and immediately forgets what kind of man he was."

A crusty old pirate with one leg, a hooked arm, and a patched eye entered a saloon in Boston. Asked about his wounds, he responded, "Fighting with Blackbeard in Charleston, I lost the leg. Fighting with Bonnet in the Caribbean, I lost the arm which was replaced with a hook." The people in the saloon asked, "How did you lose the eye?" "Well, a bird flew over and dropped some refuse in my eye," he said. "But that should not cause you to lose the eye," they responded. "I know," he said, "But I reached up to clean my eye after I had just received my new hook." He wasn't careful and lost the eye.

Carelessness in viewing Scriptures pirates our spiritual eyesight. James uses two different Greek words which translate into our English word, *look*. We will look at his second *look* in the next chapter — no pun intended. The first word, *katanoeo*, has the concept of *a casual glance.* The text says, "...he looks ...then forgets...." The reader haphazardly and hurriedly skims over Bible reading with no clear view of putting into practice what he sees.

Casual eyes towards God's word close in forgetfulness. James compares the person to one looking into a mirror who then forgets the image. The modern reader may not grasp the significance of his words. Inventors created the modern glass mirrors in the fourteenth century. In the first century people used brass mirrors. The reflection, far from being clear, required a careful gaze. Otherwise, the impression of the image soon evaporated. Dashing through the pages of the Bible leaves no lasting impression of God's image reflected back to us.

The Greek word for *listen, akroatai,* translates into our English word, *audit.* Most colleges have two fees, one for credit and a lesser fee for auditing the class. When auditing the student listens to the lectures, but does not participate in testing, grading, cramming, or writing. They only listen — no doing. While on the surface, auditing sounds great, the student invariably learns less and receives no credit on his transcript. No one gets jobs and pay raises from audited course work. The pain of doing has its rewards.

Listening and not doing God's word produces a different kind of pain — the pain of a seared conscience. Maria Cobham and Eric Cobham entered piracy during the eighteenth century. An apt pupil, Maria soon became as vicious a pirate as her husband, capturing and scuttling ship after ship. She and her husband followed a no-survivors policy. They held to an old pirate saying: "Dead cats don't mew." During their notorious career, two to three hundred innocent sailors lost their lives.

Accruing great wealth, they retired in a large estate near Le Harve on the coast of France. The unsuspecting citizens even elected Eric as magistrate. The aging pirate was now a judge! Over a 12-year period he oversaw hundreds of cases. Ironically he obtained respectability and fame for his fairness.

In spite of these advancements, guilt took its toll on Eric and Maria. Haunted by memories of her grim past, she leaped off a cliff to her death. Her suicide left her husband conscience stricken. Obsessed by the memory of his terrible deeds, he laboriously wrote a confession of all his crimes. Spending long hours in church in repentance, he had the pastor publish his detailed confession after his death. His final message to his pastor, *"Tell the people to be careful to be doers of the word!"*

35

Careful Eyes

James 1:25
"But he who looks into the perfect law of liberty and continues in it...."

The second *look* in James that we promised to look into is an intense word. The Greek word for *looks intently, parakupto,* describes a careful eye to detail. When Peter and Mary went to the garden tomb, they *looked* into the empty tomb. The same Greek word for *look* is used here. One can imagine Simon Peter stooping through the low-lying door of the tomb and staring in total amazement. That one look changed his life forever.

James though speaks of more than one look. He uses the word *parameno.* The word means to stay on course. The view into the things of God should not be a single glance, but a continuing process of gazing intently. The mind becomes quickened to the thought, "How can I put this admonition into practice?" The disciplined habit produces a doer of the word.

What are we to look intently into? James says, "...the perfect law of liberty...." Many confusions exist on the exact role

153

of the law for the child of God. The Bible makes clear that keeping the ceremonial aspects of the law does not justify a believer. Nevertheless, Jesus did not abolish the law, but fulfilled it. In Christ the core message of the law is still the will of God only taken on a different plane. James touches on the intention and attitudes that undergird the law. He pierces to the heart of the law, which is good. Psalm 19:10 speaks of the goodness of the law, "More to be desired are they than gold, yea, than much fine gold; sweeter also than honey and the honeycomb."

James speaks not just of the law but of *the law of liberty.* Empowered by grace, the child of God is not under the old law of rules and regulations. Instead, the believer lives by the power of the risen Christ. In so doing, the law is not skirted, but lived out in liberty. Paul addresses the truth in Romans 8:2, "For the law of the Spirit of life in Christ Jesus has made me free from the law of sin and death."

Pirates believed that piercing the ears and wearing an earring improved eyesight. This idea, scoffed at for centuries, has been reevaluated in light of acupuncture theory. The point on the lobe where the ear was pierced corresponds to the auricular acupuncture point controlling the eyes.[1] (Don't let your teenage son read this, though!) Whether the theory is true or not, spiritual eyes and ears are connected. Looking and listening intently to God's word improves our spiritual vision. We see more clearly through the eyes of our hearing and doing what we have heard. ***Carefulness sees more!***

---

[1]David Louis, *2201 Fascinating Facts* (New York, New York: Wings Books, 1983), p. 101.

36

The Lookout's Poem

James 1:25
"...and is not a forgetful hearer, but a doer of the work, this one will be blessed in what he does."

When I attended high school, a friend of mine wrote poetry to a girl he had feelings for. I always admired his ability with words. When the girl showed signs of disinterest, he wrote lines like: "Fortress, fortress over there, how shall I get in? I tried a dozen times or more and still you always win." The poem goes on to describe his sadness at not capturing her heart. She liked all the attention, and his poetry endeared him to her.

James uses the word *poieetai* for our English word *doing*. From this Greek word, we derive our English word *poet* and *poetry*. A poet carefully chooses each word to create his or her work. Diligence in detail adds beauty to the poem. The poet's whole personality of inner being, mind, soul, spirit, and emotion go into the creative process. Far from routine observance of commands, *poieetai* speaks of creative obedience.

A poet is one who puts words together in order to express a thought or feeling in a beautiful manner. That is what God wants us Christians to be — poets, creators of the beautiful. We are to be creative in life. We are to take all the experiences, pleasant and unpleasant, and present them as attractive poems to the world around us.[1]

How do we create the spiritual poetry of good works? The answer is to pay attention to the details of God's words in the same manner that a poet does when forming a new work. For the poet, the poem is the reward. For the child of God, doing God's word brings immense benefits. John 14:21 says, "He who has My commandments, and keeps them, it is he who loves Me. And he who loves Me will be loved by My Father, and I will love him, and manifest Myself to him." ***Doing God's word writes heaven's poems!***

---

[1]Spiros Zodhiates, *The Work of Faith* (Grand Rapids, Michigan: Zondervan, 1977), p. 105.

Section

10

Callousness

37

Mutiny on the Bounty

James 1:26-27

"If anyone among you thinks he is religious, and does not bridle his tongue, but deceives his own heart, this one's religion is useless. Pure and undefiled religion before God and the Father is this, To visit orphans and widows in their trouble, and to keep oneself unspotted from the world."

The famous *Mutiny on the Bounty* occurred on April 28, 1789. Fletcher Christian seized the *Bounty* and set Captain Bligh adrift in a 23-foot longboat with 19 loyal crewmen. Such an act of piracy warranted a formal sentence of death for all who mutinied. The British Articles of War did not play games with mutiny.

When the average person is asked the reason for the mutiny, one receives answers influenced more by Hollywood than correct facts. Even some history books take a completely biased picture against Bligh or Fletcher. The truth lies somewhere between the two extremes. The reality of the mutiny occurred because two men's weaknesses collided together after a five-month stint on the lush Tahiti island. A deadly mix of verbal insults and beautiful Tahitian women gave rise to the now famous event.

The book of James covers a similar type of mutiny — one of an unbridled tongue and uncontrolled passions. True religion bridles both. Empty religion restrains neither. The child of God can indeed at times flesh-out and find his or herself mutinying against God's highest purposes.

In the next few pages, we will search out both the *Mutiny on the Bounty* and the *mutiny of ourselves* and examine over-lapping themes. Mankind has not changed much since 1789. We may discover some fascinating information about the his-torical facts of the true *Mutiny on the Bounty* and the spiritual facts of true religion.

When someone receives Christ in America, a common ex-pression attached to them by nonbelievers is, "They got reli-gion." Hopefully they received more than mere formality. J.B. Phillips refers to religion as "rites and robes, bells and smells." James equates true religion not in terms of dead formality, but a living faith woven into the fabric of everyday living.

The Greek word for *religion, threskos,* is only used here in all of the Bible. The word refers to the outward observance of religious ceremony. James condemns an empty religion that lacks reality and positive impact.

How very easy it is for a Christian to slip into routine. We can attend Christian circles, picking up common labels, with our official green card stamped, "O.K." and still lack vibrant life. I have a pastoral friend who says his Sunday morning ser-vice is so dead it isn't worth turning the electricity on for.

Our activities can outpace our capacities to implement. A dear pastoral friend of mine who held the world record for the busiest church actually conducted six services each weekend. While visiting another church, a prophet who knew nothing of his circumstances began prophesying over him, "Thus says the Lord, you are too busy, My son. Sometimes you almost make Me tired!" In time he slowed down some and consequently enjoyed his life more.

Isaiah 1:11-13, "...The multitude of your sacrifices — O what are they to me? Says the Lord. I have more than enough of burnt offerings of rams, and the fat of fattened animals; I have no pleasure in the blood of bulls and lambs and goats. When you come to appear before Me, who has asked this of you, this trampling of My courts? Stop bringing meaningless offerings! ...They have become a burden to me; I am weary of bearing them...."

True religion impacts reality!

38

Captain Bligh

James 1:26

"If anyone among you thinks he is religious, and does not bridle his tongue, but deceives his own heart, this one's religion is useless."

Captain Bligh, the mere name conjures up images of abusive leadership. The workplace occasionally hears the name applied to a difficult boss, "He's a Captain Bligh!" We know the meaning of such a statement. The boss makes the working environment hard to endure. Was Captain Bligh and his present reputation congruent? The answer is no. To fully comprehend this man we have to first look at his strong points.

Captain Cook, considered to be the all-time greatest maritime explorer, trained young Bligh and always wrote of him positively. By the standards of the British Navy, Captain Bligh was considered lenient. At sea, captains ruled as sovereign and commonly dispensed lashings for numerous offensives. Not Bligh, he spared the lash compared to his contemporaries and even his mentor Cook. When the British government looked for a dependable leader to head the first commercial expedition in the Pacific, they chose Bligh.

After Fletcher Christian set Bligh and his loyal followers adrift in a small sailing craft, Bligh managed to sail her over 3,600 without charts and little provisions. Even Bligh's critics hail the 41-day endurance trip as the supreme example of courageous leadership. The large number of men who stood by Bligh during the mutiny, including all the officers, speaks well of him.

At the official court trial, the crewmen under oath lay the blame squarely on Christian. The court cleared Bligh of any wrongdoing. After the trial the government again chose him to lead the commercial expedition. The second trip he succeeded in the mission.

So what went wrong? Bligh's main weakness lay with his abusive tongue. He could cut a man to his innermost shame. A lashing healed quickly, but the bite of his words left permanent scars. Bligh's untamed tongue, along with Fletcher Christian's uncontrolled passions sparked the mutiny.

Each year the average person speaks over 18,000 words, enough to write 66, 800-page volumes. Proverbs 10:19 says, "In the multitude of words, sin is unavoidable." How many times have we sinned with our words? Christ says in Matthew 12:34, "Out of the overflow of the heart the mouth speaks." The abuse in Bligh's heart spilt out to his crew and caused resentment.

Imagine riding a 1,500-pound horse of restless bone and muscle without a bridle. At full gallop the ride borders more on sheer terror than leisure. The bridle harnesses all that power into useful focus. The unbridled, galloping tongue produces more damage than the largest Clydesdale running free.

A young man approached the famed philosopher, Socrates, to consider teaching him. After listening to the talkative young man, Socrates finally agreed to teach him for twice his normal fee. The young man asked, "Why the double cost?" Socrates explained that he must first teach the young man how not to talk and then he must teach him how to talk, thus the double expense.

Ephesians 4:29 says, "Let no corrupt word proceed out of your mouth, but what is good for necessary edification, that it may impart grace to the hearers."

A woman known for being a gossip confronted John Wesley with a pair of scissors and stated that his long bow tie offended her. She promptly snipped the tie, whereupon Wesley took the scissors and requested the woman stick her tongue out as its length offended him!

James 3:4 compares the tongue to the small rudder on a ship. The rudder, though small, can shape the destiny of a great vessel. In like manner the future direction of our lives proceeds from the vocal rudder. Life and death are in the power of the tongue. ***Speak to those things that are not as though they were!***

39

Mr. Christian

James 1:27
"...And to keep oneself unspotted from the world."

Born to a well-established family in England, Fletcher Christian knew the importance of high ethics. His family traced their unbroken lineage to the thirteen hundreds. For over 400 years his family remained rather prominent in British society. The Christian family name enjoyed a good reputation.

Fletcher also knew disappointment in family members. His father had died during his boyhood days. His brothers over-borrowed on the family estate and bankrupted the family. His now burdened mother faced leaving the family home for meager settings. Not alone in mutiny, Fletcher's brother, Charles, also had participated in mutiny on another ship.

A mixture of prominence and shame intersected to influence forever the life of this famous man. Not surprisingly he possessed a sensitive nature with all its strengths and weaknesses. People serving with him often found him pleasant. He could also retreat into himself and brood for hours, even days.

Once landing on the tropical paradise of Tahiti, Fletcher quickly adapted to Polynesian customs. While living on shore for five months, he adopted local dress and body tattooing. He also participated in the immoral life-style of the intoxicating island. Soon he had strong affections for a beautiful Tahitian woman he named Isabella. By the time of the *Bounty's* departure, Isabella had conceived. Now Fletcher found himself deeply torn between his duty and emotions.

On all three of Captain Cook's landings at Tahiti, he had men try to desert. Bligh also had crew members steal a longboat and flee to the tropical haven. Recapturing the deserters, Bligh loaded his crew and set sail for the West Indies. A few days back at sea, Fletcher led the mutiny and forever placed himself in the history books. In the ensuing months, over 200 men died as a direct result of the mutiny. Five months of immorality had left its mark.

James defines true religion as "keeping oneself unstained from the world." The Greek word for *keep, tereo,* indicates regular, continuous action. The influence of the world constantly makes its pull on the believer. Only a perpetual reaffirmation to purity overcomes such magnetism.

How do we keep ourselves unstained from the world? We recognize the consequences of the stains. When I visited a flea market, I vividly recall seeing a sign over some clothing, "Slightly soiled garments, price greatly reduced!" ***Sin, so alluring, always comes with a heavy price tag!***

40

The Bounty's Bible

James 1:27

"...to visit orphans and widows in their distress...."

On January 10, 1790, the *Bounty* arrived at a remote uninhabited island called Pitcairn. Seeking a permanent hideaway, the mutineers completely burned the ship. They could not turn back now. Time tested the fruit of their tree. Very quickly the idyllic hideaway disintegrated into anarchy. A combination of alcohol, lack of women to men ratio, and social abuse created turmoil.

The mutineers sought to enslave the Polynesian men for their own gain. Forced to work under harsh conditions, eventually the "blacks," as they were called, organized their own mutiny. This time bloodshed marked the occasion. The Polynesian gang chose as their first victim, Fletcher Christian. He had sown to the wind and now reaped a whirlwind. Murder swept through the entire island.

Ultimately only one mutineer remained, John Adams, along with a few Polynesian women and racially mixed children. The social experiment failed. Driven to his knees, Adams turned to the *Bounty's* Bible for spiritual guidance. With the grace of God shining on his life, he fully surrendered his life over to Christ.

The fruit of his decision changed everything. The entire island joined him in the conversion experience. What had been a social disaster, now triumphed through the ancient text of Scripture. Genuine Christian virtues replaced murder, immorality, drunkenness, and injustice. In miniature form, Pitcairn forever beaconed the need for God's word in any society. Adams, as a faithful patriarch, taught his small flock the need for true religion to be defined in our treatment of one another.

James says that true religion reflects itself in the face of attitudes and actions toward the needy. The Greek word *episkeptomai* translates into English — *to visit* or *to look after* the widows and orphans in the time of their distress. The word can be translated into the word *Bishop.* Well-known German theologian, Jurgen Moltman, says, "The coming Judge is already hidden in the least of these my brethren." Our attitude towards the least reveals the strength or weakness of our faith. ***Only through the sword of the Spirit can we slay the pirate of callousness!***

Conclusion

The city of Rome fell in 410 A.D. to barbarian hordes who unmercifully destroyed the city. The pagans went on a rampage throughout Europe. They burned churches, monasteries, and libraries. Many of the religious and educated leaders were cruelly put to death. The Dark Ages had begun.

Twenty years earlier in Britain, a family gave birth to a young man who would shine light into Europe's darkness. At a young age a group of pirates captured him and sold him into slavery in Ireland. For six years he labored under the harshest of conditions. Eventually he escaped and returned to his grateful parents in England. In many ways he had every right to resent the pagan Irish for his many mistreatments. Instead, he forgave and prayed for them.

While back with his parents, he had a vision of ministering to the Irish. To his parent's dismay their son chose to return as a missionary to Ireland. First he spent needed preparation time in study in France. With his studies completed, he then went on the great adventure of missionary work.

Arriving in Ireland, he faced many dangerous circumstances. The whole country lay in the grip of dark paganism. The light of the Gospel shone into the darkness, and the people believed. Taking the message at face value they began to send missionaries into Europe. Thomas Cahill in his excellent book, *How the Irish Saved Civilization*, credits the Irish for preserving Europe from total collapse. I think he is correct.

One young man, taken by pirates, dared to believe God was greater than pirates. God, not fickle circumstances, held his life. What the pirates meant for evil, God turned into good. The light shone in the darkness, and civilization was preserved.

We know the young man today as St. Patrick. Rome never canonized him as a saint. The common people, however, recognized his saintly life and bestowed on him the title.

Perhaps after reading this book of life's ever present pirates, you feel you have been taken hostage. Be of good cheer: God is still in control of your life. He has another chapter for you. The title is: *I Will Be With You!*

Contact

Dr. Charles H. Gaulden
200 Evangel Road
Spartanburg, South Carolina

1-864-576-8170, Extension 1219